Miss Ronaldson

Gift book of useful and ornamental knitting, netting and crochet work

Miss Ronaldson

Gift book of useful and ornamental knitting, netting and crochet work

ISBN/EAN: 9783742831989

Manufactured in Europe, USA, Canada, Australia, Japa

Cover: Foto ©Lupo / pixelio.de

Manufactured and distributed by brebook publishing software (www.brebook.com)

Miss Ronaldson

Gift book of useful and ornamental knitting, netting and crochet work

LADY'S POLKA, WITH ERMINE BORDER.

GIFT BOOK OF
USEFUL AND ORNAMENTAL
KNITTING, NETTING, AND CROCHET WORK.

The merry homes of England
Around their hearths by night
What gladsome looks of household love
Meet in the ruddy light

GIFT BOOK OF

USEFUL AND ORNAMENTAL

KNITTING, NETTING AND CROCHET WORK

By MISS RONALDSON,

> "There the wreath piles its leafy task,
> The pansies gleam, the enthodystated flower,
> Wrought gracefully into the mossy lawn,
> Unfolds its leaves; buds and leaves and sprays,
> And smiling tendrils, gracefully disposed,
> Follow the nimble fingers of the fair;
> A wreath that cannot fade, of flowers that bloom
> With sweet perfume where all breaths decay."

London:
T. NELSON AND SONS, PATERNOSTER ROW;
AND EDINBURGH.

MDCCCLV.

TO THE RIGHT HONOURABLE

LADY CHARLOTTE BERKELEY,

THIS LITTLE BOOK OF

Useful and Ornamental Knitting and Netting Work,

IS, BY PERMISSION,

MOST RESPECTFULLY DEDICATED BY

The Authoress.

PREFACE.

THE increasing attention to the subject treated of in this little Work has induced its Authoress to reduce into as simple and clear a form as possible, the voluminous and difficult instructions contained in the many able publications connected with this useful branch of polite education.

The experience of Miss Ronaldson, not only in teaching more advanced pupils, but in introducing this pleasing feminine art to beginners, has proved to her that the assortment of Patterns in Fancy Knitting and Netting, and the method of executing them now detailed and recommended, will be found an easy key to their practice. She therefore hopes, from her lengthened experience in these fancy arts, to extend, by this publication, a knowledge of them beyond the influence of her personal instructions, and to aid in providing facilities for their acquirement on the best principles, and for their easy and elegant execution.

EXPLANATION OF SIGNS

USED IN THE

KNITTING RECEIPTS.

---

1. A plain stitch.
X. Take in by knitting two stitches together.
O. Making a stitch and hole at the same time, by casting the thread over the wire.
B. Back, or pearl stitch.
S. Slip a stitch, that is, take a stitch off the wire without knitting.
S X. Slip a stitch, take in, then draw the slip one over it.
B. Take in the pearl way.

Cast Off.—Knit two stitches, draw the first over the second; knit another, draw one over the other again; so on until all are cast off.

CONTENTS

		Page
I.	Full Size Lady's Stocking,	1
II.	Shawl—Diamond Pattern for the Middle,	4
III.	Lady's Scarf.—Pattern for the Ends,	6
IV.	Pattern for Middle of Lady's Scarf,	7
V.	Pattern for Boy's Scarf,	9
VI.	A Warm Scarf or Comforter, for a Gentleman,	10
VII.	Young Lady's Scarf,	ib.
VIII.	Leaf Pattern for a Shawl,	12
IX.	Pattern for Fringe,	15
X.	Wave Pattern for a Handkerchief,	16
XI.	Band for the Throat,	18
XII.	Edging—A Small Vandyke,	20
XIII.	Edging—A Deep Vandyke,	21
XIV.	Edging—Leaf Pattern,	22
XV.	Edging,	23
XVI.	Edging,	26
XVII.	Spider-Net Trimming—With a Pretty Edge,	27
XVIII.	Edging,	29
XIX.	Edging,	30
XX.	Broad Open Edging,	31
XXI.	Coral Pattern,	33
XXII.	Simple Border for a Shawl,	34
XXIII.	Another Border,	35

CONTENTS.

		Page
XXIV.	A Wide Vandyke Edging,	34
XXV.	Simple Edge,	41
XXVI.	Narrow Pattern for an Edging,	45
XXVII.	Honiton Edge,	46
XXVIII.	Knitted Lace Border.—For Baby's Cap,	47
XXIX.	Edging with a Scallop,	52
XXX.	Edging,	56
XXXI.	Corner for a Spider-Net Handkerchief,	57
XXXII.	Broad Cuff, to wear under the Sleeve,	60
XXXIII.	Vandyke Wine-Rubber.—In Wool,	61
XXXIV.	Toilet Cover,	64
XXXV.	Toilet Cover,	70
XXXVI.	Simple Ruff for a Child,	71
XXXVII.	Baby's Hood,	72
XXXVIII.	Warm Shoe.—With Fleecy Loops in the Inside,	73
XXXIX.	Honiton Lace Cape,	76
XL.	Open Stitch for a Purse,	78
XLI.	A Pretty Strip Stitch for a Purse,	ib.
XLII.	Purse for Using up all Odd Bits of Silk,	79
XLIII.	Netted Flower-Stand.—With a Frill,	80
XLIV.	Small Netted Stand for a Glass of Flowers.—Of Berlin Wool,	81
XLV.	Another Small Netted Stand,	82
XLVI.	Netted Ribbon for the Neck,	83
XLVII.	Very Pretty Netted Scarf.—For a Tie at the Neck instead of a Handkerchief,	84
XLVIII.	Netted Cover for a Salver,	85
XLIX.	Netted Window Curtain,	86
L.	Netted Pie Napkin,	87
LI.	Round Netted Wine-Rubber,	88

CONTENTS.

		Page
LII.	Netted Wine-Rubbers,	89
LIII.	Handsome Netted Shawl,	90
LIV.	Netted Cuffs.—With a Frill,	90
LV.	A Very Pretty Netted Scarf,	91
LVI.	A Full Size Lady's Spencer,	92
LVII.	A Very Handsome Knitted Cover for a Music-Stool,	94
LVIII.	Anti-Macassars,	95
LIX.	Small Quilt,	97
LX.	Plain Black Bead-Bag,	ib.
LXI.	Bead-Bag.—The Beads in the form of a Diamond,	99
LXII.	Long Purse with Steel Beads,	101
LXIII.	Stitch for a Long Purse,	102
LXIV.	Another Stitch for a Purse more open,	103
LXV.	Spade Stitch for a Stocking,	ib.
LXVI.	Pretty Stitch for a Small Stocking or Baby's Sock,	104
LXVII.	Patterns for a Set of Wine-Rubbers,	105
LXVIII.	Diamond,	106
LXIX.	Square Pattern,	107
LXX.	Wave Pattern,	108
LXXI.	Check,	110
LXXII.	Small Check,	113
LXXIII.	Small Half Diamond,	ib.
LXXIV.	Sloping Pattern,	114
LXXV.	Broken Slope,	115
LXXVI.	Half Square,	116
LXXVII.	Large Half Diamond,	118
LXXVIII.	Oblong Pattern,	120
LXXIX.	Broken Oblong,	121
LXXX.	Napkin for a Bread-Basket,	124
LXXXI.	Polka Cap,	127

CONTENTS.

LXXXII.	Prudence Cap,	Page 130
LXXXIII.	A Simple Pattern for a Prudence Cap,	132
LXXXIV.	Neat Baby's Boots,	133
LXXXV.	Short Purse,	136
LXXXVI.	Simple Pattern for a Long Purse,	137
LXXXVII.	Leaf Pattern for a Pincushion,	138
LXXXVIII.	Lady's Cravat,	140
LXXXIX.	Warm Sole to Wear Inside the Shoe,	141
XC.	Baby's Spencer,	142
XCI.	Polka for a Child,	143
XCII.	Simple Pattern for a Collar,	148
XCIII.	Very Pretty Lace Collar,	153
XCIV.	Collar, Diamond Pattern,	154
XCV.	Point Lace Collar,	157
XCVI.	Beautiful Point Lace Collar,	159
XCVII.	Shell Pattern for a Collar,	161
XCVIII.	Handsome Netted Tippet	164
XCIX.	Long Netted Window Curtains.—For a Drawing-Room,	165
C.	Warm Cuff,	167
CI.	Sofa Cushion,	168
CII.	Shetland Handkerchief.—Same Pattern as the Sofa-Cushion,	169
CIII.	Victorine,	172
CIV.	Netted Victorine.—Green and Scarlet,	174
	Directions for Washing Shetland Work,	176
	Directions for Washing Fleecy Work,	ib.

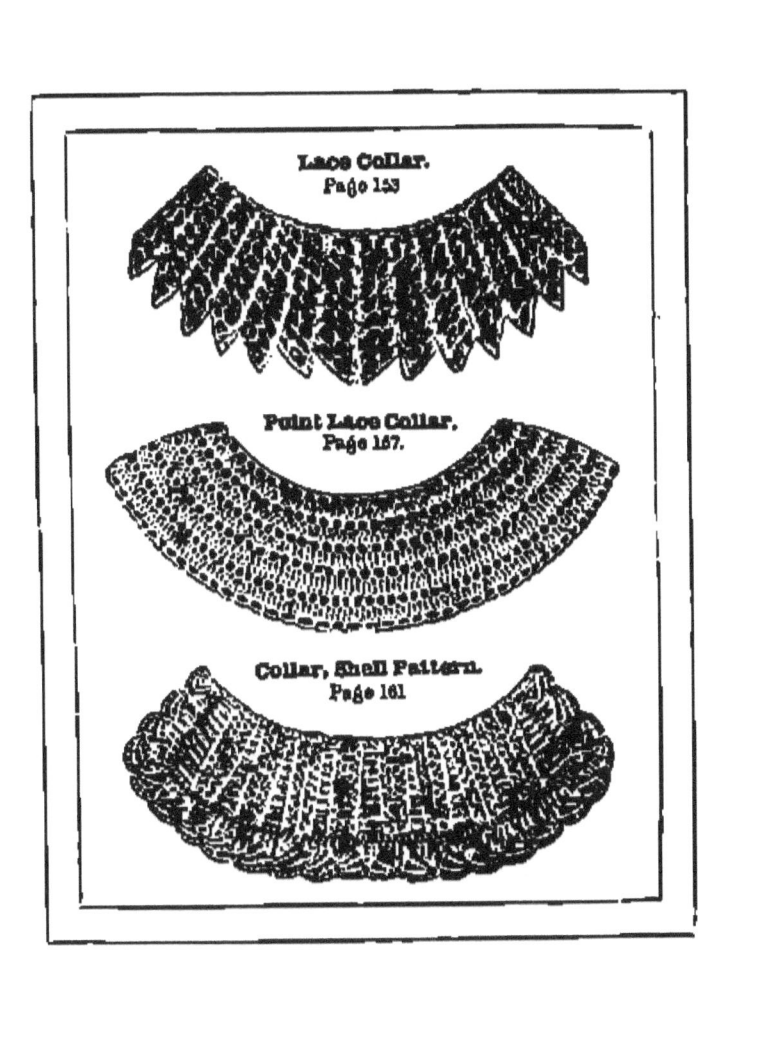

KNITTING

AND

NETTING BOOK.

I.—FULL SIZE LADY'S STOCKING.

To be knitted either in fine merino wool or white cotton; four wires, No. 18. Cast on 150 stitches, fifty on each of three wires; knit one pearl and one plain for twelve rounds; then knit plain until you have two finger-lengths done; always knitting one stitch pearl every other round for the back seam. You now take in a stitch each side of the back seam every seventh round, until you have taken in twenty-five times. You will now have 100 stitches on; knit one finger-length from where you left off taking in, which will bring you to the heel; which you knit in the following manner:—

Put twenty-five stitches on each side of the back seam, for the heel, leaving forty-nine for the instep. You knit the heel pearl every other row, always slipping your first stitch. When you have a little more than half a finger-length done, you take in on each side of the back seam every plain row, until you have taken in six on each side; you now put the heel on two wires, and fold it together on the wrong side; take a third wire, and knit off the two at the same time; when you have two knitted, you draw the one over the other; knit another stitch, then draw it over; so on until you have all the stitches taken off. You now take up every stitch along the side of the heel; knit across the instep, and take up the other side of the heel; you then, in knitting your first round, make a stitch every third stitch along each side of the heel. You now commence taking in at the instep every other round; on the first side you take in by knitting the last but one together, at the end of the side wire on the right hand side of the instep; you take in at the beginning of the wire on the left hand side by knitting your first stitch, slipping the second; knit the third stitch, then draw the slip one over it; continue taking in in the same manner until you have 100 stitches on; you then knit one fingerlength plain, which will bring you to the toe. You now commence taking in, one stitch from the beginning and end of every wire, first observing that you have an equal number on each wire;

you knit seven rounds, then take in again; then six rounds, and another take in round; then five rounds; so on until you have ten or twelve stitches left, which you take off together in the same manner as the heel.

The above proportions are good for a full size stocking. Of course, if you knit one half the size, you just reduce all parts in proportion; and if you knit the stocking with a pattern, you keep the proportions the same.

—⋅❦⋅—

IL—SHAWL.

DIAMOND PATTERN FOR THE MIDDLE.

Four skeins finest Lady Betty wool pins, No. 10.
Cast on 208 stitches, knit a plain row.
A plain row is knitted between each pattern row.

First Row.
1 1 1, O X, 1 1 1, 1 1 1, O X, 1 1 1.   Repeat.

Second Row.
1 1, O X, O X, 1 1 1 1 O X, O X 1 1.   Repeat.

Third Row.
1, O X, O X, O X, 1 1, O X, O X, O X, 1.   Repeat.

Fourth Row.
1 1, O X, O X, 1 1 1, 1 O X, O X, 1 1.   Repeat.

Fifth Row.
1 1 1, O X, 1 1 1, 1 1 1, O X 1 1 1.   Repeat.

Commence again at the first row; and you will observe, that the first and the last rows are done the same: it requires two the same to form the diamond. There are twenty-six diamonds in the width, and thirty-six in the depth of the shawl.

Border same as Receipt XXII.

In taking up the stitches for the border, you must have 250 on, which will require one stitch to be made every fourth stitch. Increase a stitch at the end of each row, so as to form a slop to sew to the other side of the border; all the increased stitches you knit plain.

III.—LADY'S SCARF.

PATTERN FOR THE ENDS.

Cast 118 stitches, knit fourteen plain rows. Seven plain at the beginning and end of each row. There are twenty-six stitches in each pattern.

First Row.

X X X X, O 1, O 1, O 1, O 1, O 1, O 1, O 1, O 1. X X X X O X. Repeat.

Second Row.
Pearl.

Commence again with first row.

If you have coloured ends, it looks well, five shades of amber, and a white strip betwixt the shades; and knit three rows between each pattern row, first a pearl, then a plain and a pearl row, changing the shades at every pattern row.

IV.—PATTERN FOR MIDDLE OF LADY'S SCARF.

Fourteen plain stitches at the beginning and end of every row.

Knit a pearl row betwixt each pattern row. There are fourteen stitches in each pattern.

After knitting the last pattern in the row, knit

O X O X, before the fourteen plain, so that both edges may be the same.

First Row.
O, X O X O X O X 1 1 1, 1 1 1.   Repeat.

Second Row.
O X O X 1 O X O X 1 1 1, 1 1.   Repeat.

Third Row.
O X O X 1 1 O X O X 1 1 1, 1.   Repeat.

Fourth Row.
O X O X 1 1 1 O X O X 1 1 1,   Repeat.

Fifth Row.
O X O X 1 1 1, 1 O X O X 1 1.   Repeat.

Sixth Row.
O X O X 1 1 1, 1 1, O X O X 1.   Repeat.

Seventh Row.
O X O X 1 1 1, 1 1 1, O X O X.   Repeat.

Eighth Row.

O X O X 1 1 1, 1 1 1, 1 O X 1.
Commence again at first row.

V.—PATTERN FOR BOY'S SCARF.

Cast on forty-five stitches, knit a plain row.

Knit six stitches plain at the beginning; five plain at end of each row; knit O X 1 O X 1 O X 1 the same every row, always observing that the O is above the O in the last row, which will form an open stripe. It requires two skeins of four ply fleecy; pins No. 8. Finished with fringe, knotted in.

VI.—A WARM SCARF OR COMFORTER

FOR A GENTLEMAN.

Cast on sixty stitches; slip the back way O X O S X O S X O S X; so on to the end of the row, every row the same. Finish by sewing on a fringe. It takes three skeins four-ply fleecy, or if white, three skeins of six-ply Lady Betty wool. Pins No. 8.

VII.—YOUNG LADY'S SCARF.

Cast on eighty-four, knit two plain rows.

First Row.

B X X X O 1 O 1 O 1 O 1 O X X X. Repeat four times. Knit six plain at the beginning, and six plain at end of each row.

Second Row
Pearl.

Third Row.
Plain.

Fourth Row.
Pearl;
always remembering to knit the first and last six plain; and in the back row, knit the B stitch plain; and in the plain, knit it B: there will be five B stitches in all. Take four shades of scarlet, two skeins of each change at every pattern row; put one white, then the four scarlets again, then another white, until you have three stripes of scarlet, then a pattern, and the three rows of white, which forms the end. Knit six plain rows; the middle is a stripe 1 1 1 O X 1 1 1 O X, the same every row; always observing that

your Os are opposite one another; when, as long as required, knit the end to correspond with the other.

VIII—LEAF PATTERN FOR A SHAWL.

Begin at the back corner.
Cast on three stitches, work a pearl row betwixt each pattern row.

First Row.
S O 1 O 1.

Second Row.
S O 1 1 1 O 1.

Third Row.
S O 1 1 1, 1 1 O 1.

Fourth Row.
S O 1 1 1, 1 1 1, 1 O 1.

Fifth Row.
S0111,111,111,01.

Sixth Row.
S0111,110101111101.

Seventh Row.
S01X111011101111X101.

Eighth Row.
S011X110111,11011X1101.

Ninth Row.
S0111X10111,111,101X11101.

Tenth Row.
S01111X0111,111,111,0X111101.

Eleventh Row.
S01111101[01111XX11101]01 111101.

Twelfth Row.

S O 1 X 1 1 1 0 1 1 1 [O 1 1 1 X X 1 1 0 1 1 1]
O 1 1 1 X 1 O 1.

Thirteenth Row.

S O 1 1 X 1 1 [O 1 1 1 1 1 O 1 1 X X 1 O 1 1 1 1 1]
O 1 1 X 1 1 O 1.

Fourteenth Row.

S O 1 1 1 X 1 O 1 1 1, 1 1 1, 1 O [1 X X O 1 1 1,
1 1 1, 1 O] 1 X 1 1 1 O 1.

Fifteenth Row.

S O 1 1 1 1 X O 1 1 1, 1 1 1, 1 1 1, O [X O 1 1 1,
1 1 1, 1 1 1 O] X 1 1 1 1 O 1.

Commence again at the eleventh row.

Repeat the pattern within the brackets as many times as there are leaves: they will increase gradually. When they are as large as you wish, cast off, and then take up both sides at one time; and whatever pattern you work for the border, let out at each corner, and the back.

The following makes a pretty border:—

First Row.

B X X X, O 1, O 1, O 1, O 1, O 1, O X X X, B.

Second Row.

B 1 1 1, 1 1 1, 1 1 1, 1 1 1, 1 1 1, 1 1 B.

A pearl row betwixt each pattern row. When deep enough, which will depend on the size of the shawl, cast off, and sew on the fringe.

IX.—PATTERN FOR FRINGE.

Cast on six stitches, O X O X O X, always working the back way, every row the same; sew it on, and wash the shawl before taking down the fringe, which causes it to be curled; take down four stitches, and commence to do so where you ended.

X.—WAVE PATTERN FOR A HANDKERCHIEF.

Begin at the back. Cast on three stitches.

First Row.
S 0 1 0 1.

Second Row.
S 0 1 1 1 0 1.

Third Row.
S 0 1 1 0 X 1 1 0.

Fourth Row.
S 0 1 1 1 0 X 1 1 0 1.

Fifth Row.
S O 1 1 1, 1 O X 1 1 1 O 1.
Sixth Row.
S O 1 1 1, 1 1 O X 1 1 1, 1 O 1.
Seventh Row.
S O 1 1 O X 1 1 O X 1 1 O X 1 O 1.
Eighth Row.
S O 1 1 1 O X 1 1 O X 1 1 O X 1 1 O 1.
Ninth Row.
S O 1 1 1 1 O X 1 1 O X 1 1 O X 1 1 O 1.
Tenth Row.
S O 1 1 O X 1 1 O X 1 1 O X 1 1 O X 1 1 O 1.

The first wave will now be formed, and the first hole of the second. Continue O X 1 1 every pattern row; always observing that when the wave lies to the left, you O when you pass the O; when
o

it lies to the right, you O *before* the O in the last row. Do seven holes to the right, and seven holes to the left.

When large enough, cast off; then take up both sides of the border. On the side of a shawl there ought to be three-fourths of the number of stitches that are on the neck when finished.

In knitting the border, let out at each corner, both front and back.

XL.—BAND FOR THE THROAT.

Cast on twenty stitches, on No. 16 wires.

Two wires and six skeins of Berlin wool are required.

Knit plain, and increase one at the end of each row, until you have thirty-one on: The pattern is—

First Row.
S, then O X O X to the end.

Second Row.
Plain.

Third Row.
Pattern same as first.

Fourth Row.
Plain.

Fifth Row.
Same as first.

Sixth Row.
Plain.

Seventh Row.
Same as first.

Knit four plain rows, then commence again at

the first row; so on until long enough; and knit a plain piece to finish, taking in at the end of each row, until twenty stitches are left; cast them off; fasten with a loop and button.

XII.—EDGING—A SMALL VANDYKE.

Cast on nine stitches, and knit a plain row.

First Row.
S 1 1 0 X O O X O O X.

Second Row.
O 1 1 D 1 1 D 1 1 O X 1.

Third Row.
S 1 1 O X 1 1 1, 1 1 1, 1.

Fourth Row.
Cast off three, knit 1 1 1, 1 1 O X 1.
Repeat from the first row

XIII.—EDGING—A DEEP VANDYKE.

Cast on seven stitches, and knit a plain row.

First Row.
S 1 1 O X O O X.

Second Row.
O 1 1 B 1 1 O X 1.

Third Row.
S 1 1 O X 1 1 1, 1 1.

Fourth Row.
1 1 1, 1 1 1, O X 1.

Fifth Row.
S 1 1 O X O O X O O X.

Sixth Row.
1 1 B 1 1 B 1 1 O X 1.

Seventh Row.
S 1 1 O X 1 1 1, 1 1 1.

Eighth Row.
1 1 1, 1 1 1, 1 1 O X 1.

Ninth Row.
S 1 1 O X O O X O O X O O X.

Tenth Row.
1 1 B 1 1 B 1 1. B 1 1 O X

Eleventh Row.
S 1 1 O X 1 1 1, 1 1 1, 1 1 1.

Twelfth Row.
Cast off seven stitches, knit 1 1 1 O X 1.
This finishes one vandyke.
Commence again at the first row.

XIV.—EDGING—LEAF PATTERN.

Cast on ten stitches, knit one plain row.

First Row.
8 1 1 0 X O O X O O X 1.

Second Row.
1 1 1 B 1 1 B 1 1 1, 1 1.

Third Row.
8 1 1 0 X 1 1 0 O X O O X 1.

Fourth Row.
1 1 1 B 1 1 D 1 1 1, 1 1 1, 1.

Fifth Row.
8 1 1 0 X 1 1 1, 1 0 0 X O O X 1.

Sixth Row.
1 1 1 B 1 1 B 1 1 1, 1 1 1, 1 1 1.

Seventh Row.
8110X111,111,00X00X1.

Eighth Row.
111B11B111,111,111,11.

Ninth Row.
8110X111,111,1100X00X1.

Tenth Row.
111B11B111,111,111,111,1.

Eleventh Row.
8110X111,111,111,111,11 1.

You have now twenty stitches on; cast off ten, and knit plain to the end of the row.

One leaf will now be formed.

Commence again at the first row.

XV.—EDGING.

Cast on seven stitches, knit a plain row.

First Row.
8 1 1 0 X O O X

Second Row.
O 1 1 B 1 1 0 X 1.

Third Row.
8 1 1 0 X 1 1 1, 1.

Fourth Row.
1 1 1, 1 1 1 0 X 1.

Fifth Row.
8 1 1 0 X O O X O O X

Sixth Row.
1 1 B 1 1 B 1 1 0 X 1.

Seventh Row.
8 1 1 0 X 1 1 1, 1 1 1.

Eighth Row.
Cast off four, knit 1 1 1 0 X 1.
One vandyke will now be formed.
Commence again at the first row.

XVL—EDGING.

Cast on eleven stitches, knit one plain row.

First Row.
1 1 1 0 X 0 0 X 0 0 X 0 0 X.

Second Row.
1 1 B 1 1 B 1 1 B 1 1 0 X 1.

Third Row.
1 1 1 O X 1 1 1, 1 1 1, 1 1 1.

Fourth Row.
Cast off three stitches, knit 1 1 1, 1 1 1, 1 O X 1.
Commence again at the first row.

XVII.—SPIDER NET TRIMMING,
WITH A PRETTY EDGE.

Cast on fifteen stitches, knit two plain rows.

First Row.
1 1 1, O S X O 1 1 1, O X O O X O O X.

Second Row.
O, 1 L, B, 1 1, B, 1 B B B, B B B, 1 O X 1.

Third Row.
1 1 1, 0, X, 0, X, 1, X, 0, 1 1 1, 1 1 1, 1 1.

Fourth Row.
Cast off three stitches, 1 1 1, 1, B B B, B B B, 1 0 X 1.

Fifth Row.
1 1 1, 0, X, 1, 0, 8 X, 0, 1 1, 0 0, X, 0 0, X.

Sixth Row.
0 1 1, B, 1 1, B, 1, B B B, B B B, 1, 0, X, 1.

Seventh Row.
1 1 1, 0, X X, 0, 1, 0, X, 1 1 1, 1 1 1, 1 1.

Eighth Row.
Cast off three stitches, 1 1 1, 1, B B B, B B B, 1 0 X 1.

Commence again at first row.

XVIIL—EDGING.

Cast on twelve stitches. Knit a plain row between each pattern row.

First Row.
O X 1 O X O 1 1 1, 1 O X 1.

Second Row.
O X 1 O X O X O 1 1 1 O X 1.

Third Row.
O X 1 O X O X O 1 1 O X 1.

Fourth Row.
O X 1 O X O X O X O X O 1 O X 1.

Fifth Row.
O S X O X O X O X O X X O X 1.

Sixth Row.
O S X O X O X O X 1 1 O X 1.

Seventh Row.
O S X O X O X 1 1 1 O X 1.

Eighth Row.

O 8 X O X O 1 1 1, 1 O X 1.

Commence again at first row.

XIX.—EDGING.

Cast on eleven stitches.

First Row.

8 1 1, O X O O, X O O, X O O, X.

Second Row.

1 1 B, 1 1 B, 1 1 B, 1 1 O, X 1.

Third Row.

8 1 1 O X, 1 1 1, 1 1 1, 1 1 1.

Fourth Row.

1 1 1, 1 1 1, 1 1 1, 1 1, O X 1.

Fifth Row.

S 1 1, O X, 1 1 1, 1 1 1, 1 1 1.
Cast off three, and 1 1 1, 1 1 1, 1, O X 1.
Commence again at first row.

XX.—BROAD OPEN EDGING

Cast on eleven stitches.

First Row.
S 1 1, O O, X, O O, X, O O X, O O X.

Second Row.
1 1 B 1 1 B, 1 1 B, 1 1 B, 1 1 1.

Third Row.
S 1 1, (O O X. Repeat from parenthesis to the end of the wire.

Fourth Row.
1 1 B, 1 1 B, 1 1 B, 1 1 B, 1 1 D, 1 1 D, 1 1 L.

Fifth Row.
8 1 1, (O O X. Repeat to the end.

Sixth Row.
1 1 B nine times; the last three plain.

Seventh Row.
8 1 1, (O O X. Repeat; the last stitch plain.

Eighth Row.
1 1 1 B, (1 1 B. Repeat; last three plain.

Ninth Row.
8 1 1. Take in twenty times.

Tenth Row.
Cast off four stitches. Take in eight times; plain two.
Commence again at first row.

XXX.—CORAL PATTERN.

Cast on seventeen stitches in each pattern row.

First Row.

1 1 1, 1 1 X, 1 1, 0 X, 0 X, 0, 1, 0, 1 1 X, 1 1 1 1, X 1 1 0, X 0, X, 0 1 0, 1 1 X.

Second Row.

X 1 1, X 1 1, 0 X, 0 X, 0, 1 1 1, 0, 1 1, X, 1 1 X, 1 1, 0, X 0, X 0, 1 1 1, 0, 1 1 1.

Third Row.

X X, 1 1, 0, X 0, X 0, 1 1 1, 1 1 0, 1 1 X, X 1 1, 0 X, 0 X, 0 1 1 1, 1 1 0, 1 1 1.

Fourth Row.

X 1 1, 0 1, 0 X, 0 X, 0 1 1, X, 1 1 1 1, X, 1 1, 0 1, 0 X, 0 X, 0 1 1, X 1 1 1, 1 1.

Fifth Row.
1 1 1, 0, 1 1 1, 0, X, 0, X, 0, 1 1 X, 1 1 X, 1 1, 0, 1 1 1, 0 X, 0 X, 0, 1 1, X 1 1, X.

Sixth Row.
1 1 1, 0 1 1 1, 1 1 0 X, 0, X 0, 1 1 X X 1 1 0 1 1 1, 1 1 0, X 0, X 0, 1 1 X X.

A pearl row betwixt each pattern row.

XXII.—SIMPLE BORDER FOR A SHAWL.

First Row.
1, 0, 1 1 1 1, X, 1 1 1, 1 1 1, X, 1 1 1 1, 0, 1. Repeat.

Second Row.
D, D, O, B D B D, $\overset{M}{D}$, B D B D, $\overset{M}{D}$, D D D B, O, D B.

Third Row.
1 1 1, 0, 1 1 1, X, 1 1, X, 1 1 1 1, 0, 1 1 1.

Fourth Row.

D D B B, O B B D D, D̄, D̄, D B B B, O, D B B B.

XXIII.—ANOTHER BORDER.

Sixteen stitches on each pattern.

First Row.
X X O 1 O 1 O 1 X X O X O X. Repeat.

Second Row.
Pearl.

Third Row.
1 1 1, 1 1 1, 1 1 1, 1 1 1, O X O X.

Fourth Row.
Pearl.

Commence again at first row.

XXIV.—A WIDE VANDYKE EDGING

Cotton, No. 40; wires, No. 22.
Cast on fourteen stitches, knit one plain row.

First Row.
1 1 1, 1, O, X, 1, O, X, O, X, O, X 1.

Second Row.
1 1 1, 1 1 1, 1 1 1, 1, O, X, 1 1.

Third Row.
1 1 1, 1, O, X, 1 1 1, 1 1 1, 1 1.

Fourth Row.
1 1 1, 1 1 1, 1 1 1, 1, O, X, 1 1.

Fifth Row.
1 1 1, 1, O, X, 1 1, O, X, O, X, O, 1 1.

Sixth Row.
1 1 1, 1 1 1, 1 1 1, 1 1, O, X, 1 1.

Seventh Row.
1 1 1, 1, 0, X, 1 1 1, 1 1 1, 1 1 1.

Eighth Row.
1 1 1, 1 1 1, 1 1 1, 1 1, 0, X, 1 1.

Ninth Row.
1 1 1, 1 0, X, 1 1 1, 0, X, 0, X, 0, 1 1.

Tenth Row.
1 1 1, 1 1 1, 1 1 1, 1 1 1, 0, X, 1 1.

Eleventh Row.
1 1 1, 1, 0, X, 1 1 1, 1 1 1, 1 1 1, 1.

Twelfth Row.
1 1 1, 1 1 1, 1 1 1, 1 1 1, 0, X, 1 1.

Thirteenth Row.
1 1 1, 1, 0, X, 1 1 1, 1, 0, X, 0 X, 0, 1 1.

Fourteenth Row.
1 1 1, 1 1 1, 1 1 1, 1 1 1, 1, 0, X, 1 1.

Fifteenth Row.
1 1 1, 1, 0, X, 1 1 1, 1 1 1, 1 1 1, 1 1.

Sixteenth Row.
1 1 1, 1 1 1, 1 1 1, 1 1 1, 1, 0, X, 1 1.

Seventeenth Row.
1 1 1, 1, 0, X, 1 1 1, 1 1, 0, X, 0, X 0 1 1.

Eighteenth Row.
1 1 1, 1 1 1, 1 1 1, 1 1 1, 1 1, 0, X, 1 1.

Nineteenth Row.
1 1 1, 1, 0, X, 1 1 1, 1 1 1, 1 1 1, 1 1 1.

Twentieth Row.
1 1 1, 1 1 1, 1 1 1, 1 1 1, 1 1, 0, X, 1 1.

Twenty-First Row.
1 1 1, 1, 0, X, 1 1 1, X, 0, X, 0, X 0, X 1.

Twenty-Second Row.
1 1 1, 1 1 1, 1 1 1, 1 1 1, 1, 0, X, 1 1.

Twenty-Third Row.
1 1 1, 1, 0, X, 1 1 1, 1 1 1, 1 1 1, 1 1.

Twenty-Fourth Row.
1 1 1, 1 1 1, 1 1 1, 1 1 1, 1, 0, X, 1 1.

Twenty-Fifth Row.
1 1 1, 1 0, X, 1 1, X, 0, X, 0, X, 0, X 1.

Twenty-Sixth Row.
1 1 1, 1 1 1, 1 1 1, 1 1 1, 0, X, 1 1.

Twenty-Seventh Row.
1 1 1, 1, 0, X, 1 1 1, 1 1 1, 1 1 1, 1.

Twenty-Eighth Row.
1 1 1, 1 1 1. 1 1 1, 1 1 1, O, X, 1 1.

Twenty-Ninth Row.
1 1 1, 1, O, X, 1, X, O, X, O X, O X 1.

Thirtieth Row.
1 1 1, 1 1 1, 1 1 1, 1.1, O, X, 1 1.

Thirty-First Row.
1 1 1, 1, O, X, 1 1 1, 1 1 1, 1 1 1.

Thirty-Second Row.
1 1 1, 1 1 1, 1 1 1, 1 1, O, X, 1 1.

Thirty-Third Row.
1 1 1, 1, O, X, X, O, X, O, X, O, X, 1.

Thirty-Fourth Row.
1 1 1, 1 1 1, 1 1 1, 1, O, X, 1 1.

KNITTING AND NETTING BOOK.   41

Thirty-Fifth Row.
1 1 1, 1, O, X, 1 1 1, 1 1 1, 1 1.

Thirty-Sixth Row.
1 1 1, 1 1 1, 1 1 1, 1, O, X, 1 1.

One vandyke will now be formed.
Commence again at first row.

XXV.—SIMPLE EDGE.

Cast on twelve stitches, knit two plain rows.

First Row.
1 1 1, O, X, 1, O, X, O, X, O X.

Second Row.
1 1 1, 1 1 1, 1 1 1, O, X 1.

Third Row.
1 1 1, O, X, 1 1, O, X, O X O 1.

Fourth Row.
1 1 1, 1 1 1, 1 1 1, 1, O, X, 1.

Fifth Row.
1 1 1, O, X, 1 1 1, O, X, O X O 1.

Sixth Row.
1 1 1, 1 1 1, 1 1 1, 1 1, O X 1.

Seventh Row.
1 1 1, O, X, 1 1 1, 1, O, X, O, X, O, 1.

Eighth Row.
1 1 1, 1 1 1, 1 1 1, 1 1 1, O X 1.

Ninth Row.
1 1 1, O X 1 1 1, 1 1, O, X, O X O 1.

Tenth Row.
1 1 1, 1 1 1, 1 1 1, 1 1 1, 1, O, X, 1.

Eleventh Row.
1 1 1, O X 1 1 1, 1 1 1, O X O X O 1.

Twelfth Row.
1 1 1, 1 1 1, 1 1 1, 1 1 1, 1 1, O X 1.

Thirteenth Row.
1 1 1, O, X 1 1 1, 1 1, X O X O X O 1.

Fourteenth Row.
1 1 1, 1 1 1, 1 1 1, 1 1 1, 1 1, O, X 1.

Fifteenth Row.
1 1 1 O X 1 1 1 1 X O X O X O X

Sixteenth Row.
1 1 1, 1 1 1, 1 1 1, 1 1 1, 1 O X 1.

Seventeenth Row.
1 1 1 0 X 1 1 1 X O X O X O X.

Eighteenth Row.
1 1 1, 1 1 1, 1 1 1, 1 1 1, O X 1.

Nineteenth Row.
1 1 1 0 X 1 1 X O X O X O X.

Twentieth Row.
1 1 1, 1 1 1, 1 1 1, 1 1 0 X 1.

Twenty-First Row.
1 1 1, 0 X 1 X O X O X O X.

Twenty-Second Row.
1 1 1, 1 1 1, 1 1 1, 1, O, X, 1.

Twenty-Third Row.
1 1 1, 0, X, X O X O X O X.

Twenty-Fourth Row.

1 1 1, 1 1 1, 1 1 1, O X 1.

Commence again at first row.

XXVL—NARROW PATTERN FOR AN EDGING.

Cast on seven stitches, knit two plain rows.

First Row.

1 1 1, O X O O X.

Second Row.

O, 1 1, B, 1 1 O X 1.

Third Row.

1 1 1, O X 1 1 1, 1.

Fourth Row.

Cast off two, 1 1 1, O X 1.

Commence again at first row.

XXVII.—HONITON EDGE.

Cast on seven stitches; wires, No. 20.

First Row.
1 1 1, 1 1 0 0 X.

Second Row.
0 1 1 D 1 1 1, 1 1.

Third Row.
1 1 1, 1 1 1, 1 1 1.

Fourth Row.
1 1 1, 1 1 1, 1 1 1.

Fifth Row.
1 1 1, 1 1, 0 0 X 0 0 X.

Sixth Row.
1 1, B 1 1, B 1 1 1, 1 1.

Seventh Row.
1 1 1, 1 1 1, 1 1 1, 1 1.

Eighth Row.
1 1 1, 1 1 1, 1 1 1, 1 1.

Cast off four stitches, plain seven.

XXVIII.—KNITTED LACE BORDER,

FOR BABY'S CAP.

Cotton, Taylor's, No. 40; wires, No. 22.
Cast on thirty-two stitches, work two plain rows.

First Row.
S 1 1 1, 1 1 O S X O 1 1 1, 1 1 O X 1 1 1, 1 1 1 O X 1 1 1, 1 1 1, 1 1.

Second Row.
S 1 D D D, B B, X B O B B B, B D X B O B B B, X O D B B, O X D B B 1.

Third Row.

S11X0111,110X11011X111,1011X
111,111.

Fourth Row.

S1BBBXBBB0BBBXBDD0BSXOB
BB,BBB,B0XB1.

Fifth Row.

SX01110SX01110X01111X1101
111X1111.

Sixth Row.

S1BXBBB,BB0BXBBB,BB0BB0X
BBB,BBX0BB1.

Seventh Row.

S1110X111X0111,111,111,X0111
111,X011.

Eighth Row.

S 1 O D X D B B, D B, O B X B B B, B B D, B D B, O X B X O B D B, D l.

Ninth Row.

S 1 1 1, 1 1 O S X O 1 1 1, 1 1 1, 1 1 1, X 1 1 O 1 1 1 1 X 1 1 O 1 1.

Tenth Row.

S 1 O D B D, X D D D O B D D X B B B, B B B, X O D D B O X D B B l.

Eleventh Row.

S 1 1 X O 1 1 1, 1 1 O X 1 1 1, 1 X 1 1 1, 1 O 1 1 X 1 1 1 1 O 1 1.

Twelfth Row.

S 1 O D B D, D B, X D O D B B, D B X B D X O D B B, D B D, B O X D l.

Thirteenth Row.

S X O 1 1 1 O S X O 1 1 1, O X O X 1 1 1, 1 1 1, O
X 1 1 1, 1 1 1, 1 1.

Fourteenth Row.

S 1 B B B, B B X B O B B B, D B X B O B B O X
B B B, B B X O B B 1.

Fifteenth Row.

S 1 1 1 O X 1 1 1 X O 1 1 1, O 1 1 X 1 1 1 1 O 1 1 X
1 1 1, 1 1 1.

Sixteenth Row.

S 1 B B B, X B B B, O B D B, X B B B, O B B B, B
O X B X O B D B, B 1.

Seventeenth Row.

S 1 1 1, 1 1 O S X O 1 1 1, 1 1 O 1 1 1, 1 X 1 1 O 1 1
1, 1 X 1 1 1 1.

Eighteenth Row.

S1BXBBB,BBOBXBBB,BBOBBB,X
OBBBOXBBB1.

Nineteenth Row.

S11X0111,11OX111,111,11X0111,
111,X011.

Twentieth Row.

S1O,BXBBB,BBOBXBBB,BDB,XOB
BD,BBB,DOXD1.

Twenty-First Row.

SX0111,OSX0111,OX111,1X11011
1,1X11011.

Twenty-Second Row.

S1OBBB,XBBB,OBBB,XBB,BBBOX
BBB,BBXOBB1.

Twenty-Third Row.

S 1 1 1, O X 1 1 1, X O 1 1 1, 1 1 X 1 1 1 1 O 1 1 X 1 1 1 1 O 1 1.

Twenty-Fourth Row.

S 1 O B D B, D B X B O D B B, D D X B B B, D D O X D X O B D B D 1.

Commence again at the first row.

———

XXIX.—EDGING WITH A SCOLLOP.

Cast on eleven stitches.
Cotton, Taylor's, No. 40; wires, No. 22.

First Row.

S, 1 1, O, X, 1, O, X, O, X, O, 1.

Second Row.

1 1 1, 1 1 1, 1 1 1, O, X, 1.

KNITTING AND NETTING BOOK.

Third Row.
8, 1 1, 0, X, 1 1, 0, X, 0, X, 0, 1.

Fourth Row.
1 1 1, 1 1 1, 1 1 1, 1, 0, X, 1.

Fifth Row.
8, 1 1, 0, X, 1 1 1, 0, X, 0, X, 0, 1.

Sixth Row.
1 1 1, 1 1 1, 1 1 1, 1 1, 0, X, 1.

Seventh Row.
8, 1 1, 0, X, 1 1 1, 1, 0, X, 0, X, 0 1.

Eighth Row.
1 1 1, 1 1 1, 1 1 1, 1 1 1, 0, X, 1.

Ninth Row.
8, 1 1, 0, X, 1 1 1, 1 1, 0, X, 0, X, 0, 1.

Tenth Row.

1 1 1, 1 1 1, 1 1 1, 1 1 1, 1, O, X 1.

Eleventh Row.

S, 1 1, O, X, 1 1 1, 1 1 1, O, X, O, X, O, 1.

Twelfth Row.

1 1 1, 1 1 1, 1 1 1, 1 1 1, 1 1, O, X, 1.

Thirteenth Row.

S, 1 1, O, X, 1 1 1, 1 1 1, X X X.

Fourteenth Row.

X, X, X, 1 1 1, 1 1, O, X, 1.

Commence again at the first row.

XXX.—EDGING.

Somewhat similar to the last, but a little broader.

Cast on fourteen stitches.

First Row.
1 1 1, O, X, 1, O, X, O, X, O, X, O, X.

Second Row.
O, 1 1 1, 1 1 1, 1 1 1, 1 1, O, X 1.

Third Row.
1 1 1, O X 1 1 O X O X O X O X.

Fourth Row.
O 1 1 1, 1 1 1, 1 1 1, 1 1 1, O, X, 1.

Fifth Row.
1 1 1, O, X 1 1 1 O X O X O X O X.

Sixth Row.
0, 1 1 1, 1 1 1, 1 1 1, 1 1 1, 1, 0, X, 1.

Seventh Row.
1 1 1 0 X 1 1 1 1, 0 X 0 X 0 X 0 X.

Eighth Row.
0 1 1 1, 1 1 1, 1 1 1, 1 1 1, 1 0 X 1.

Ninth Row.
1 1 1 0 X 1 1 1, 1 1 0 X 0 X 0 X 0 X.

Tenth Row.
0 1 1 1, 1 1 1, 1 1 1, 1 1 1, 1 1 1, 0 X 1.

Eleventh Row.
1 1 1 0 Y 1 1 1, 1 1 1. Lift the second stitch of the left hand wire over the first one, then the third, &c., until six be taken off; then two will remain, which O X.

Twelfth Row.
0 1 1 1, 1 1 1, 1 1 1, 1 1 0 X 1.

XXXL—CORNER FOR A SPIDER-NET HANDKERCHIEF.

Cast on three stitches.
Let out one at each side, until you have nine stitches on, then form the border as follows:—
Knit a pearl row betwixt each pattern row.

First Row.
8 1 0 X 0 1 0 X 0 1 1.

Second Row.
8 1 0 X 0 1 1 1 0 X 0 1 1.

Third Row.
8 1 0 X 0 1 1 1, 1 1 0 X 0 1 1.

Fourth Row.

S 1 0 X 0 1 1 1, 1 1 1, 1 0 X 0 1 1.

Fifth Row.

S 1 0 X 0 1 1 1, 1 1 1, 1 1 1, 0 X 0 1 1.

Sixth Row.

S 1 0 X 0 1 1 1, 1, (0 1 0) 1 1 1, 1 0 X 0 1 1.

Seventh Row.

S 1 0 X 0 1 1 1, 1 (0 1 1 1 0) 1 1 1, 1 0 X 0 1 1.

Eighth Row.

S 1 0 X 0 1 1 1, 1 1 (0 1 0 X 1 X 0 1 0) 1 1 1, 1 0 X 0 1 1.

Ninth Row.

S 1 0 X 0 1 1 1, 1 X (0 1 1 1 0 S X 0 1 1 1 0) X 1 1 1 1 0 X 0 1 1.

Tenth Row.

S1OXO111,1(OXOX1XO1OX1XOXO)
111,1OXO11.

Eleventh Row.

S1OXO111,11(O1110SXO1110SX
01110)111,110XO11.

Twelfth Row.

S1OXO111,1(OXOX1XO1OX1XO1O
X1XOXO)111,1OXO11.

Thirteenth Row.

S1OXO111,11(O1110SXO1110SX
O1110SXO1110)111,110XO11.

Fourteenth Row.

S1OXO1111(OX1XO1OX1XO1OX1
XO1OX1XOX)111,1OXO11.

Repeat between the parentheses as your work increases.

XXXII.—BROAD CUFF

TO WEAR UNDER THE SLEEVE.

Cast on fifty-eight stitches.
Knit four plain at beginning and end of every row.

First Row.
1 1, X, O 1 O, X 1 1.   Repeat.

Second Row.
1 X, O, 1 1 1, O, X, 1.   Repeat.

Third Row.
X, O, 1 1 1, 1 1, O, X.   Repeat.

Fourth Row.
1 1, O, X 1 X, O, 1 1.   Repeat.

Fifth Row.
1 1 1, O  X O, 1 1 1.   Repeat.

A plain row betwixt each pattern row.
Knit an edging, and sew to the wrist.

XXXIII.—VANDYKE WINE RUDDER,
IN WOOL.

Five skeins of Berlin wool will be required; one deep blue, two amber, and two pink, make a pretty contrast. Two wires, No. 16.

Cast on twenty-seven stitches.

The S in this pattern must be slipped off the pearl way.

First Row.
O S X eight times, then 1 O O X.

Second Row.
O 1 1 B 1, O S X, O S X, O S X, which will leave fifteen stitches on the wire, then turn to knit the third row.

Third Row.
O S X, O S X, O S X, 1 1 1, 1 1.

Fourth Row.
1 1 1, 1 1 0 8 X, 0 8 X, 0 8 X, 0 8 X, which will leave twelve on, then turn.

Fifth Row.
0 8 X, 0 8 X, 0 8 X, 0 8 X, 1 0 0 X 0 0 X.

Sixth Row.
1 1 B 1 1 B 1, 0 8 X, 0 8 X, 0 8 X, 0 8 X, 0 8 X, which will leave nine, then turn.

Seventh Row.
0 8 X, 0 8 X, 0 8 X, 0 8 X, 0 8 X, 1 1 1, 1 1 1, 1.

Eighth Row.
1 1 1, 1 1 1, 1 (0 8 X, six times, which will leave six, then turn.

Ninth Row.
0 8 X, six times, 1 0 0 X 0 0 X 0 0 X.

Tenth Row.
1 1 B, 1 1 B, 1 1 B, 1, (O S X seven times, which will leave three, then turn.

Eleventh Row.
O S X, seven times, 1 1 1, 1 1 1, 1 1 1, 1.

Twelfth Row.
Cast off seven stitches, knit two plain, then O S X eight times.

Change the colour, and commence the pattern. It takes seventeen patterns to form the round. When done, cast all off, and sew it together.

A good way to arrange the colours:—Begin with the blue, dark amber, light amber, blue, dark pink, light pink; same again.

The above Receipt makes a very pretty wine-rubber, knitting in fine Dutch twist, and fine wires, No. 18; but you require to cast on forty-one stitches; knit in the same manner as the last, only do not turn on the second row until you have four additional O S X. Continue knitting until you have four or five more vandykes, then the Berlin wool one; you will see when it is large enough when the round is formed; then sew it together.

XXXIV.—TOILET COVER.

Knitted in diamonds, and sewed together.
Cast on three stitches with Dutch twist; wires, No. 10; knit a plain row.
A plain row betwixt each pattern row.

First Row.

1 1 0 1.

KNITTING AND NETTING BOOK.   65

Second Row.
1 1 0 1 1.

Third Row.
1 1 0 1 0 1 1.

Fourth Row.
1 1 1, 0 1 0, 1 1 1.

Fifth Row.
1 1 1, 0 1 1 1, 0 1 1 1.

Sixth Row.
1 1 1, 0 1 1 1, 1 1, 0 1 1 1.

Seventh Row.
1 1 1, O, seven plain, then O 1 1 1.

Eighth Row.
1 1 1 O, nine plain, then O 1 1 1.

F

Ninth Row.
1 1 1 O, eleven plain, then O 1 1 1.

Tenth Row.
1 1 1 O, thirteen plain, then O 1 1 1.

Eleventh Row.
1 1 1 O, fifteen plain, then O 1 1 1.

You now knit a pearl row between each pattern row.

Twelfth Row.
1 1 1 O, seventeen plain, then O 1 1 1.

Thirteenth Row.
1 1 1 O, nineteen plain, then O 1 1 1.

Fourteenth Row.
1 1 1 O, twenty-one plain, then O 1 1 1.

Fifteenth Row.

1 1 1 O, twenty-three plain, then O 1 1 1.

A plain row between each pattern row.

Sixteenth Row.

1 1 1 O, twenty-five plain, then O 1 1 1.

Seventeenth Row.

1 1 1 O, twenty-seven plain, then O 1 1 1.

Eighteenth Row.

1 1 1 O, then O X to the end, but the last two plain.

Nineteenth Row.

1 1 1 X, twenty-five plain, then X 1 1 1.

Twentieth Row.

1 1 1 X, twenty-three plain, then X 1 1 1.

Twenty-First Row.
1 1 1 X, twenty-one plain, then X 1 1 1.

Now a pearl row between each row.

Twenty-Second Row.
1 1 1 X, nineteen plain, then X 1 1 1.

Twenty-Third Row.
1 1 1 X, seventeen plain, then X 1 1 1.

Twenty-Fourth Row.
1 1 1 X, fifteen plain, then X 1 1 1.

Now a plain row between each row.

Twenty-Fifth Row.
1 1 1 X, thirteen plain, then X 1 1 1.

Twenty-Sixth Row.
1 1 1 X, eleven plain, then X 1 1 1.

Twenty-Seventh Row.
1 1 1 X, nine plain, then X 1 1 1.

Twenty-Eighth Row.
1 1 1 X, seven plain, then X 1 1 1.

Twenty-Ninth Row.
1 1 1 X, five plain, then X 1 1 1.

Thirtieth Row.
1 1 1 X, three plain, then X 1 1 1.

Thirty-First Row.
1 1 1 X 1 X 1 1.

Thirty-Second Row.
1 1 1 X X 1 1.

Thirty-Third Row.
1 1 X X 1.

Thirty-Fourth Row.
1 X X
Cast off

XXXV.—TOILET COVER.

Cast on twenty-one stitches for each pattern.
A pearl row betwixt each pattern row.

First Row.
X, 1 1 1, X, 1 0 1, 0 1, X, 1 1 1, X, 1 0 1, 0 1 1.
Repeat.

Second Row.
X, 1 X, 1 0, 1 1 1, 0 1 X 1 X 1 0 1 1 1, 0 1 1.
Repeat.

Third Row.
8 X, 1 0, 1 1 1, 1 1 0 1, 8 X, 1 0 1 1 1, 1 1, 0 1 1.
Repeat.

Fourth Row.
1 1 0, 1 0, 1 X, 1 1 1, X, 1 0 1 0 1 X 1 1 1 X.
Repeat.

Fifth Row.
1 1 0, 1 0 1, 1 1 X, 1 X, 1 0 1 1 1, 0 1 X 1 X.

Sixth Row.
1 1 0 1 1 1, 1 1 0, 1 8 X 1 0 1 1 1, 1 1 0 1 8 X.

XXXVI.—SIMPLE RUFF FOR A CHILD.

Garter stitch. White and blue double Berlin.
Pins, No. 6.
Cast on fifty stitches.

Knit four rows of white, then four of blue, until you have five strips of white and five of blue; cast off, and fold it together, adding strings.

XXXVII.—BABY'S HOOD.

Cast on eighty stitches; Pins, No. 7.
Two skeins four-ply Lady Betty wool will be required.

Knit eighty rows plain to roll up for the front, then a row O X O X, six plain rows, then cast on ten stitches at each end for the back of the neck, another row O X O X, then two plain rows, then knit twenty rows of 1 O X 1 O X 1 O X; repeat, for the crown part.

Sew up the back, draw in the crown with a needle, and add a silk button, line it with satin, draw in two ribbons in the O X rows, finish with a rosette of same ribbon.

Eighty stitches are cast on for the curtain, which is knitted the same pattern as the crown.

XXXVIII.—WARM SHOE,

WITH FLEECY LOOPS IN THE INSIDE.

Four skeins four-ply fleecy wool, two white and two scarlet, two wires, No 12, will be required.

Cast on thirteen stitches for the toe, of scarlet wool, knit four plain rows; fifth row, knit a loop of white in at every other stitch at the same time with the scarlet, but put the white round the first finger of the left hand before you put it round the wire, to make the loop; sixth row plain, next a row with loops, then knit five plain rows, then a row putting in the white loops, another plain row, and then a row with loops, then five plain rows. The whole shoe done in the same manner. Knit twenty-seven rows, making a stitch at the beginning and end of every fourth row, until you have forty-five on; you will now be at the instep; you will then knit fifteen stitches only on each side; when long enough, cast off; you judge the length by the size you wish your shoe; take up the stitches round the instep, and knit the first row plain, next pearl, then plain and pearl again, next a row of holes, then a plain row and a pearl row, cast off, sew up the heel and in the sole, draw a ribbon through the holes, get a thin leather sole put on.

The sole is knitted in the same manner as the shoe. Cast on thirteen stitches at the toe, let out a stitch at each side for the broad part, and take in again at the narrow and let out again for the hool.

XXXIX.—HONITON LACE CAPE.

The finest black Lady Betty wool; Pins, No. 9.
Cast on 200 stitches.
Knit eight plain rows.

First Row.

1 1 O X. Repeat, knitting four stitches plain at the beginning and end of the row.

Second Row.

Plain; commence again at first row. When you have knitted six pattern rows, commence taking in a stitch at the end of every row.

When you think it a proper depth, cast off ten

stitches at the commencement of every row, till only fifty remain, which cast off.

An edge to be knitted of the following pattern, which is to be sewed all round.

Cast on ten stitches.

First Row.
S, 1 1, O, X 1 O X O O X.

Second Row.
O 1 1 B 1 1 O X 1 O X 1.

Third Row.
S 1 1 O X 1 O X 1 1 1, 1.

Fourth Row.
1 1 1, 1 1 1, O X 1 O X 1.

Fifth Row
S, 1 1 O X 1 O X O O X O O X.

Sixth Row.
1 1, B, 1 1, B 1 1 0 X 1 0 X 1.

Seventh Row.
8 1 1 0 X 1 0 X 1 1 1, 1 1 1.

Eighth Row.
1 1 1, 1 1 1, 1 1 0 X 1 0 X 1.

Ninth Row.
1 1, 0 X 1 0 X 1 1 1, 1 1 1.

Tenth Row.
Cast off four stitches, 1 1 1, 0 X 1 0 X 1.

Commence again at first row; the cape is finished by drawing a ribbon in at the neck, the vandyke falling over.

XL.—OPEN STITCH FOR PURSE.

Cast on fifty stitches; two wires, No. 18. Two skeins purse twist; knit two plain rows.

Pattern, O X O X O. Repeat.

Every row the same, but always knitting the pearl way. When long enough, sew up a third at each end. This stitch requires to be well stretched.

XLI.—A PRETTY STRIP STITCH FOR A PURSE.

Cast on sixty-six stitches; knit two plain rows.
Pattern, 8 1 1 O X 1 O X 1 O X 1 O X. Repeat. Ending with a plain stitch. Every row the same, always observing that the stitch which is knitted plain is the one that has been cast up

in the previous row. When done, sew up a third part at each end.

It requires three skeins purse twist; two wires, No. 16 or 18.

All purses ought to be stretched, which is done in the following manner: pin them out on any thing soft, wet a cloth and lay on, then iron above the damp cloth; leave it to dry.

This stitch will also make a pretty leg to a baby's boot.

— ⚹ —

XLII.—PURSE FOR USING UP ALL ODD BITS OF SILK.

Cast on sixty-eight stitches; knit two plain rows

First Row.

X X X 0 1 0 1 0 1 0 1 0 1 0 X X X.

Commence again; knit three pearl rows betwixt each pattern row. Change the silk at every pattern row.

Any colours can be used, and every strip may be different.

XLIII.—NETTED FLOWER-STAND,

WITH A FRILL

Four shades of pink, and four shades of green, with white.

Cast on 180 loops with the white, a medium size mesh, net five rows; then take your darkest pink and net forty-five loops, putting four loops into each loop of white, then your next shade, and net other forty-five loops in the same manner; then your third shade, net forty-five the same, then the lightest, and net the last forty-five in the same way. Net four pieces the same, two of them with the pink, and two with the green. Fold each piece into four and draw it up, and sew it on a quarter of the stand, then the other three on in the same manner. You make the stand of a bit of pasteboard, covered with green or pink silk; a round piece a finger-length in diameter.

XLIV.—SMALL NETTED STAND FOR A GLASS OF FLOWERS.

OF BERLIN WOOL.

Cast on fourteen loops on a medium size mesh, then take a small one, and net three rounds, then take the widest mesh and net four loops into every other loop; you miss a loop without netting any into it; then take the fine mesh and net four rounds; then net six loops, and turn and net five loops, leaving the last of the six unnetted; then turn and net four loops; turn and net three loops; then two loops; then one. You now tie on your wool, and net another six loops in the same manner as the last six loops, ending with one, and so on till you have vandykes all round.

———❊———

XLV.—ANOTHER SMALL NETTED STAND.

Cast on fifty loops with a dark shade of amber and a mesh an inch broad, then take a very small mesh and net two rounds; change the shade and net three rounds with the same mesh; then take a mesh a size larger, and the next shade of wool, and net three rounds, then net three rounds with the same mesh, of blue wool; you then take the broad mesh and net three loops into every loop for the fringe—with blue also.

XLVI.—NETTED RIBBON FOR THE NECK.

Seven shades of amber, one skein of each shade, and three of white, with three additional skeins of the middle shade, will be required. No. 10 mesh.

Cast on 100 loops with white; net four rows; then one row of each shade, commencing with the lightest, go on to the darkest, then back to the lightest, then four rows of white; then net two loops into each one of the middle shade, on each side, then take a wide mesh and net three loops into one at each end to finish.

XLVII.—VERY PRETTY NETTED SCARF,
FOR A TIE AT THE NECK, INSTEAD OF A HANDKERCHIEF.

You require three shades and white of berlin wool.

Cast on 150 loops with a mesh, say the size of No. 10; net three rows of the darkest shade and three of the next shade, then three of the lightest; you then take a broad mesh and net one row, then a row taking three loops together, and net other two loops into the ones you have taken together; so on in the whole row. You then take your small mesh again and net twelve rows; you then take the broad mesh and net a row; then a row taking the three together the same way as before; you now take the lightest shade and net three rows;

then three rows with the next; then the darkest shade, and net three rows. You draw the ends together and add tassels.

XLVIII.—NETTED COVER FOR A SALVER.

Cast on twelve loops with white cotton, a mesh about half an inch broad; take a small mesh and net two rows; then take the broad mesh and net two loops into each loop; then take the small mesh and net three rounds; take the broad mesh again and net two loops into every one; then the small mesh and net twelve rounds. You now commence the vandyke: you net eight loops, then turn and net seven; turn and net six; turn and net five; turn and net four; turn and not three; then two, and then one. Cut off the cotton and tie it on to the row, and net the vandykes all round in the same manner.

XLIX.—NETTED WINDOW CURTAIN.

Coarse Dutch twist; two meshes a half an inch broad; another an inch and a half broad will be required.

Cast on eighty loops with the small mesh, and net fifteen rows; take the broad mesh and net one row; then a row taking three loops into one; then another row putting three loops into every loop; you then take the small mesh and net other fifteen rows; then take the wide mesh and net three rows in the same manner as the last three with the wide one; you then net other fifteen with the narrow one; then three with the wide one in the same manner as last three; then fifteen with the narrow one. Now take the wide one and net four loops into every other loop; then a mesh half the width of the smallest one, and net two rows; then take the one you netted all the fifteen rows with, and net a loop into every other one—which forms the scallop at the bottom.

L.—NETTED PIE NAPKIN.

Cast on forty loops with Dutch twist on a medium size mesh; net five rounds; put two loops into every loop of the sixth round; then net fourteen rounds; put two loops into every loop of the next round; then net twenty rounds of *round* netting; then take a small mesh and net five rounds; then take the large mesh and net twenty rounds of the round netting; then net a round, taking two loops together every time; then fourteen rounds; another round taking two loops together; then five rounds, which completes it. Draw the ends together and push them into each other so as to form two puffs.

Note, The only difference between the plain and round netting is, that before passing the needle through the loop on the work, you reverse it and take up the loop backwards.

LI.—ROUND NETTED WINE RUBBER.

Cast on twenty loops on a medium size mesh, take a fine one and net three rounds; join it together at the first fine round; take the larger mesh; net a round putting two loops into every one; then the fine one again, net four rounds; then take the large one; net a round putting two loops into every one; then take the fine one again and net six rounds, then take a very broad mesh, say an inch and a half broad, and net a round putting three loops into every one, for the fringe. You take a needle and darn in two holes all round on the last six done with the fine mesh.

LII.—NETTED WINE RUBBERS.

Cast on forty loops on a small mesh; net a square; fill in with darning; any pattern, according to taste, forming circles or diamond for a border, and a few spots in the centre; sew a fringe round to finish.

LIII.—HANDSOME NETTED SHAWL.

Six shades of purple and one white of double Berlin; one ounce of each is required.

Cast on seventy-seven loops; net two rows of each shade, beginning with the dark and ending with the white; commence again with the dark and net eleven stripes, then fold it across, and net it together, putting two stitches into every third stitch; when within ten loops of the back corner, put three stitches into every corner, that is ten on each side of the corner, with the darkest shade; net three rows of each shade; net three stitches into each of white, with a broad mesh.

LIV.—NETTED CUFFS, WITH A FRILL.

Two colours; four skeins of each is required;

a mesh the size of gauge No. 10, and one twice that size.

Cast on thirty loops with the small mesh; net thirty rows; take the broad mesh and put two loops into every one; then a row with the fine one; then another row with the broad, putting two into every one again; you then net two rows with the fine one, which finishes the frill; net thirty rows and the two edge rows of the same colour; net a frill to the other side in the same manner; sew it together, and turn one frill down over the other.

LV.—A VERY PRETTY NETTED SCARF.

It will require seven shades of scarlet Berlin, four skeins of each shade.

A mesh about an inch broad, and one No. 5 or 6. Cast on 130 loops with the broad mesh, and using the wool double of the darkest shade; then net two rows with the small mesh, using the wool single.

Commence again with the large mesh, and so on till your shades are done; then commence with the second lightest, then the next shade, ending with the dark, which completes the scarf; the ends are then drawn up, and a tassel added.

LVI.—A FULL SIZE LADY'S SPENCER.

Cast on 110 stitches; Pins No. 8.

Four skeins Lady Betty Wool will be required. Knit two plain rows; then a row of holes; throw up a stitch eighteen stitches from each end on every other row, to form the gusset for the front, until there are twenty stitches increased at each side; then continue knitting on the seventy-four middle stitches, leaving an equal number at each end for the fronts; knit thirty-five rows, which will make it deep enough for the back; then continue knitting taking in a stitch at every row to form the shoulder, until you have only forty on the pin, which cast off; then commence one of the fronts; knit forty-four rows; cast off two stitches at the outer edge, knitting the remainder of the row; continue doing so till you have twenty-four stitches on, which cast off and sew to the shoulder; then commence the other front, which knit the same.

FOR THE SLEEVE.

Cast on thirty stitches; knit twelve rows: one stitch pearl and one stitch plain; then knit twelve plain rows; continue plain, letting out every fifth row until you have seventy stitches on; cast off four at the beginning of every row until it is brought to a point; sew up the sleeve and join it to the spencer; draw in a ribbon at the neck and waist.

LVII.—A VERY HANDSOME KNITTED COVER FOR A MUSIC-STOOL.

Six different colours of shaded wool, say pink, blue, amber, green, purple and scarlet; betwixt each stripe of the shaded wool put a stripe of a plain colour; dark claret looks well.

Cast on ninety stitches; Pins No. 11.

First Row.
O S X, to the end of the row.

Second Row.

O 8 X, eighteen times; then knit the eighteen back again; commence again and knit nineteen; then turn and knit the nineteen back again the same as you did the eighteen; go on in the same manner knitting an additional O 8 X, at the end of every second row until you come to a point; one stripe will now be formed; knit twenty-four stripes, changing the colour at every stripe.

Cast off all excepting twelve stitches; then sew it together, pulling down the twelve for a fringe; tie the fringe of every stripe into a tassel with blue.

LVIII.—ANTI-MACASSARS

Are pretty knitted of coloured Lady Betty wool;

four shades of blue, and four of amber, with white betwixt.

Cast on 108 stitches; Pins No. 10.

Knit four plain rows.

First Row.

X X X X O 1 O 1 O 1 O 1 O 1 O 1 O 1 O X X
X X D. Repeat to the end.

Second Row.
Pearl.

Third Row.
Plain.

Fourth Row.
Pearl.

Knit four stitches plain at the beginning and end of each row; always observe and knit the pearl stitch plain on the pearl row.

Change the colour at every *first* row.

LIX.—SMALL QUILT.

Cast on five stitches for each pattern.
Double Berlin wool; Pins No. 9.

First Row.

O, S, 1 1, pass the S over the two plain, O, S, 1, pass the S over the 1 plain.

Second Row.

Pearl.

Commence again at first row.
This quilt is prettiest when knitted with white wool and lined with rose colour.

LX.—PLAIN BLACK DEAD-BAG.

Four skeins purse twist will be required; string

on the beads before commencing; two wires No. 18. Cast on from forty to fifty stitches, according to the size you wish. Knit two plain rows; next row knit a stitch and put forward a bead to the end of the row; a plain row betwixt every bead row; so on until you have rather more than a quarter of a yard knitted; and with two plain rows cast off. Sew up the two sides and add a fringe, which is done by fastening your thread to the edge of the bag at the top of the side; string on about twenty beads, then fasten them to the side; string on about twenty-four for the next loop; so on increasing a few beads every loop until you come to the bottom; then continue them all the same length, and make the two sides correspond.

You can either add a top or draw it with rings.

LXI.—BEAD-BAG.

THE BEADS IN THE FORM OF A DIAMOND.

Cast on sixty-one stitches; wires No. 18. Four skeins purse twist will be required; knit three plain rows.

First Row.

1 1 1,·(1 1 1 1 1 1·1 1 1 1 1·1 1 1 1 1 1;
Repeat from parenthesis.

Second Row.
Plain.

Third Row.
1 1·(1 1 1 1·1 1 1 1·1 1 1 1·1 1 1 1·1 1 1 1·.
Repeat from parenthesis.

Fourth Row.
Plain.

Fifth Row.
Same as first.

Sixth Row.
Plain.

Seventh Row.
Plain.

Eighth Row.
Plain.

Ninth Row
1 1 1 1 1 1 · 1 1 1 1 1 1 ·. Repeat.

Tenth Row.
Plain.

Eleventh Row.
1 1 1 1 1 · () 1 1 1 · 1 1 1 1 · 1 1 1 1 · Repeat.

Twelfth Row.
Plain.

Thirteenth Row.

Same as ninth row.

Three plain rows.

Commence again at first row.

The bead is put forward at every dot.

When you have knitted a little more than a quarter of a yard, cast off, and sew up the sides; add a fringe as in the former pattern.

LXII.—LONG PURSE WITH STEEL BEADS.

Cast on sixty stitches; wires No. 18.

Knit a plain row; a bead is placed between the plain stitches in every alternate row.

First Row.

8 1 O X (1 1 O X 1 1 O X. Repeat.

Second Row.

S, 1 1 O X, 1 1 O X 1 1. Repeat.

Commence again with first row.

Sew up a third at each end; draw up the ends and add rings and a tassel at one end; sew the other flat with a fringe of beads.

LXIII.—STITCH FOR A LONG PURSE.

Cast on forty-nine stitches; knit a plain row Pattern: S 1 O X 1 O X 1 O X; same to the end of the row, every row the same, always observing to put the Os above one another. Three skeins of purse twist and two wires No. 18 are required; sew up one third at each end.

LXIV.—ANOTHER STITCH FOR A PURSE MORE OPEN.

Cast on forty stitches; knit a plain row.

Pattern: 1 1 O X O X 1 1 O X O X, so on to the end of the row, every row the same, always knitting the back way. Two skeins of purse twist and two wires No. 20 are required; sew up one third at each end.

LXV.—SPADE STITCH FOR A STOCKING.

132 stitches in all; ten stitches in each pattern; nine patterns in the whole stocking; work one plain row between each pattern row.

First Row.
X 1 1 O 1 1 O 1 1 X B.

Second Row.

X 1 0 1 1 1 1 0 1 X B.

Third Row.

X O 1 1 1, 1 1 1, O X B.

Fourth Row.

1 0 1 1 X X 1 1 0 1 B.

Fifth Row.

1 1 0 1 X X 1 0 1 1 B.

Sixth Row.

1 1 1, O X X O 1 1 1 B.

LXVI.—PRETTY STITCH FOR A SMALL STOCKING OR BABY'S SOCK.

Cast on any number of stitches that can be

divided by 5; knit six rows pearl and plain at top.

First Row.
B 1 O X 1 D 1 O X 1 B.

Second Row.
1 B B B B 1 B D B B 1.

Third Row.
B 1 1 O X B 1 1 O X B.

Fourth Row.
Same as second row.

Commence again at first row; if four wires are used, the second row is knitted B 1 1 1 1 B 1 1 1 1 B all round.

LXVII.—PATTERNS FOR A SET OF WINE-RUDDERS.

Cast on seventy-four stitches on each; knit ten plain rows at the commencement, and ten at the end of each, and seven plain stitches at the beginning and end of every row, on each rubber; they are finished with a fringe.

LXVIII.—DIAMOND.
First Row.
1 1 1 1 (B 1 1 1, 1 1 1, 1 1 1. Repeat from parenthesis.

Second Row.
B B B, (1 1 1 B B B, B B B, B. Repeat from parenthesis.

Third Row.
1 1 B, (B B, B B, 1 1 1, 1 1. Repeat from parenthesis.

Fourth Row.
B (1 1 1, 1 1 1, 1, B B B. Repeat from parenthesis.

Fifth Row.
B, B, B, B, B, B, B, D B 1. Repeat.

Sixth Row.
1 1 1, 1 1 1, 1 1 1, B. Repeat.

Seventh Row.
1 (B B B, B B B, B, 1 1 1. Repeat from parenthesis.

Eighth Row.
1 1 1, B B B, 1 1 1, 1. Repeat.

Ninth Row.
B B B (1 B B B, B B B, B B B. Repeat from parenthesis. Commence again.

—✠—

LXIX.—SQUARE PATTERN.
Six plain and six pearl alternately, until you

have eight rows knit; you then commence the row with pearl, and knit six pearl and six plain for other eight rows; then commence with the plain again; and so on until you have it large enough.

LXX.—WAVE PATTERN.

First Row.

Four pearl, then four plain alternately.

Second Row.

Five pearl, then four plain and four pearl to the end, ending with three pearl.

Third Row.

Two plain, then four pearl and four plain alternately, ending with two pearl.

Fourth Row.

Three plain, then four pearl and four plain alternately, ending with one pearl.

Fifth Row.

Same as the first row.

Sixth Row.

Same as the fourth row.

Seventh Row.

Same as the third row.

Eighth Row.

One plain, then four pearl and four plain alternately, ending with three pearl.

Ninth Row.

Four plain and four pearl to the end. Commence again at the second row.

LXXI.—CHECK.

You only cast on seventy-one for this pattern.

First Row.
Pearl.

Second Row.
Plain.

Third Row.
Pearl.

Fourth Row.
Plain.

Fifth Row.
Three pearl and six plain. Repeat.

Sixth Row.
Three plain and six pearl. Repeat.

Seventh Row.
Three pearl and six plain. Repeat.

Eighth Row.
Three plain and six pearl. Repeat.

Ninth Row.
Three pearl and six plain. Repeat.

Tenth Row.
Three plain and six pearl. Repeat.

Eleventh Row.
Three pearl and six plain. Repeat.

Twelfth Row.
Three plain and six pearl. Repeat.

Commence again at the first row.

LXXII.—SMALL CHECK.

First Row.
Two plain and two pearl. Repeat.

Second Row.
Same again.

Third Row.
Two pearl and two plain. Repeat.

Fourth Row.
Same as third row.
Commence again at the first row.

LXXIII.—SMALL HALF DIAMOND.

First Row.
Five pearl and one plain. Repeat.

Second Row.
Three pearl and three plain.   Repeat.

Third Row.
Five plain and one pearl.   Repeat.

Fourth Row.
Three plain; (one pearl and five plain.   Repeat from parenthesis.

Fifth Row.
One pearl; (three plain and three pearl.   Repeat from parenthesis.

Sixth Row.
One plain and five pearl.   Repeat.

Seventh Row.
Same as the sixth.

Eighth Row.

Two pearl; (three plain and three pearl. Repeat from parenthesis.

Ninth Row.

Two plain; (one pearl and five plain. Repeat from parenthesis.

Commence again at the fourth row.

LXXIV.—SLOPING PATTERN.

First Row.

Three pearl and three plain. Repeat.

Second Row.

One plain; (three pearl and three plain. Repeat from parenthesis.

Third Row.

Two pearl; (then three plain and three pearl. Repeat from parenthesis.

Fourth Row.
Three plain and three pearl. Repeat.

Fifth Row.
Two plain; (then three pearl and three plain.
Repeat from parenthesis.

Sixth Row.
Two pearl; (then three plain and three pearl.
Repeat from parenthesis.
Commence again at the first row.

LXXV.—BROKEN SLOPE.

First Row.
Three pearl and three plain. Repeat.

Second Row.
Two pearl; (then three plain and three pearl.
Repeat from parenthesis.

Third Row.
Two plain; then three pearl and three plain. Repeat.

Fourth Row.
Three plain and three pearl. Repeat.
Commence again at the first row.

LXXVI.—HALF SQUARE.

First Row.
One plain and nine pearl. Repeat.

Second Row.
Eight plain and two pearl. Repeat.

Third Row.
Three plain and seven pearl. Repeat.

Fourth Row.
Six plain and four pearl. Repeat.

Fifth Row.
Five plain and five pearl. Repeat.

Sixth Row.
Four plain and six pearl. Repeat.

Seventh Row.
Seven plain and three pearl. Repeat.

Eighth Row.
Two plain and eight pearl. Repeat.

Ninth Row.
Nine plain and one pearl. Repeat.

Tenth Row.
Pearl row.

Commence again at the first row.

LXXVII.—LARGE HALF DIAMOND.

First Row.
Nine pearl and one plain. Repeat.

Second Row.
Two pearl; (seven plain and three pearl. Repeat from parenthesis.

Third Row.
Two plain; (then five pearl and five plain to the end.

Fourth Row.
Four pearl; (three plain and seven pearl. Repeat from parenthesis.

Fifth Row.
Four plain; (one pearl and nine plain. Repeat from parenthesis.

Sixth Row.

Five plain; (one pearl and nine plain. Repeat from parenthesis.

Seventh Row.

Three pearl; (three plain and seven pearl. Repeat from parenthesis.

Eighth Row.

Three plain; (then five pearl and five plain to the end.

Ninth Row.

One pearl; (seven plain and three pearl. Repeat from parenthesis.

Commence again at the first row.

LXXVIII.—OBLONG PATTERN.

Cast on four additional stitches for this pattern, which will make seventy-eight.

First Row.

Eight plain and eight pearl to the end.

Second Row.

Eight plain and eight pearl to the end.

Third Row.

Eight plain and eight pearl to the end.

Fourth Row.

Eight plain and eight pearl to the end.

Fifth Row.

Eight pearl and eight plain to the end.

Sixth Row.
Eight pearl and eight plain to the end.

Seventh Row.
Eight pearl and eight plain to the end.

Eighth Row.
Eight pearl and eight plain to the end.
Commence again at the first row.

LXXIX.—BROKEN OBLONG.

This pattern also requires seventy-eight stitches to be cast up.

First Row.
Eight pearl and eight plain to the end.

Second Row.
Eight pearl and eight plain to the end.

Third Row.
Eight pearl and eight plain to the end.

Fourth Row.
Eight pearl and eight plain to the end.

Fifth Row.
Four plain; then eight pearl and eight plain to the end.

Sixth Row.
Four pearl; then eight plain and eight pearl to the end.

Seventh Row.
Four plain; then eight pearl and eight plain to the end.

Eighth Row.
Four pearl; then eight plain and eight pearl to the end.

Ninth Row.

Eight plain and eight pearl to the end.

Tenth Row.

Eight plain and eight pearl to the end.

Eleventh Row.

Eight plain and eight pearl to the end.

Twelfth Row.

Eight plain and eight pearl to the end.

Thirteenth Row.

Four pearl; then eight plain and eight pearl to the end.

Fourteenth Row.

Four plain; then eight pearl and eight plain to the end.

Fifteenth Row.

Four pearl; then eight plain and eight pearl to the end.

Sixteenth Row.

Four plain; then eight pearl and eight plain to the end.

Commence again at the first row.

LXXX.—NAPKIN FOR A BREAD-BASKET.

Wires No. 16; fine Dutch Twist.

Cast on 186 stitches; there are nine stitches in each pattern. This pattern looks well for a stocking or pincushion.

First Row.

B B B, X, 1 1 1, 1 1 1, 1 B B B, O 1 O. Repeat.

KNITTING AND NETTING BOOK. 125

Second Row.
1 1 1, B D B, 1 1 1, B D B, B B B̃, B Repeat.

Third Row.
B D B, X 1 1 1, 1 1, B D D, 1 0 1 0 1. Repeat.

Fourth Row.
1 1 1, B D D, D B̃ 1 1 1, B D B, B B. Repeat.

Fifth Row.
B B B, X, 1 1 1, B B B, 1 1, 0 1 0 1 1. Repeat.

Sixth Row.
1 1 1, B B, D̃, 1 1 1, B B B, B B B, B. Repeat.

Seventh Row.
B B B, X 1, B B B, 1 1 1, 0 1 0 1 1 1. Repeat.

Eighth Row.
1 1 1, D̃, 1 1 1, B D D, B B B, B B B. Repeat.

Ninth Row.

B B B, O, 1, O, B B B, X, 1 1 1, 1 1 1, 1. Repeat.

Tenth Row.

1 1 1, D B B, 1 1 1, B B B, B D B, B. Repeat.

Eleventh Row.

D D B, 1, O, 1 O 1 D D D, X 1 1 1, 1 1. Repeat.

Twelfth Row.

1 1 1, B B D, B D, 1 1 1, B B B, B B. Repeat.

Thirteenth Row.

B B B, 1 1, O, 1, O, 1 1, D B B, X 1 1 1. Repeat.

Fourteenth Row.

B B, 1 1 1, O 1, O 1 1 1, B B B, B 1. Repeat.

Fifteenth Row.

1 1 1, B B B, B D B, B B B, 1 1 1, X. Repeat.

LXXXI.—POLKA CAP.

Two colours of Shetland Wool; Pins No. 9.
Cast on eighty-six stitches

First Row.
Plain.

Second Row.
Pearl.

Third Row.
Holes by working O X O X.

Fourth Row.
Plain; change the colour this row.

Fifth Row.
Pearl.

Sixth Row.
Same as the third row.

Seventh Row.
Plain.

Eighth Row.
Pearl.

Ninth Row.
Same as the third row.

Same pattern throughout the cap; always change the colour the first plain row after having done three rows of holes of the same colour. When you have done twelve rows of holes, continue with the same colour, and leave twenty-four stitches at each end, and continue the middle part until you have twelve rows of holes; then knit out to the end of the twenty-four stitches that were left; continue the row of holes, the plain row and the pearl row, until you have four more rows of holes;

then change the colour and work four plain rows for an edge; cast it off, which forms the back part of the cap; draw the part that was knitted in the middle, which forms the caul of the cap; knit the border separately, and sew it on.

BORDER.
Cast on thirty stitches.

Knit the same pattern as the cap, which is a plain row, a pearl row, and a row of holes; knit eleven rows of holes in one colour, and twelve rows of holes in the other colour; sew it on the cap to form two puffs; the part with twelve rows of holes is folded together, and goes next the face; the part with the eleven rows of holes is then folded, and forms the upper half. Knit the same for the two puffs on the other side; make six flowers with the wool, and sew three on each side betwixt the puffs. The flowers are made by making a fringe and rolling it round a stalk made of a different colour.

The space on the front of the cap betwixt the two puffs is finished by a broad plaiting made of the worsted, and sewn on; plait strings, and draw a string on each side below the part that forms the caul, and tie them behind, drawing the cap into the size of the head; draw another string down the middle of the cap to tie under the chin; put a tassel at the end of each string.

LXXXII.—PRUDENCE CAP.

Cast on 100 stitches, Pins No. 0.

First Row.
Plain.

Second Row.
Pearl.

Third Row.
Row of holes O X.

Fourth Row.
Pearl.

Fifth Row.
Plain. Knit the two last stitches together; continue to do so.

Sixth Row.
Change the colour and pearl the row.

Seventh Row.
Plain.

Eighth Row.
Pearl.
Commence again at the third row.

When you have nine strips knitted, cast off; then take up the sides and knit one strip and take off; take up the other side and do the same; hem down half a strip all round the cap; draw a ribbon or a plaited string in the back part, and tie behind, and another down the front to tie under the chin.

It requires six skeins of white Berlin wool, and ten skeins of pink, and two yards of ribbon.

LXXXIII.—A SIMPLE PATTERN FOR A PRUDENCE CAP.

Cast on 100 stitches.

Work three plain rows; change the colour; knit a row of holes O X; knit three plain rows; so on, knitting the two last stitches together in every row; knit seven rows when you commence the eighth strip; take up the sides and knit a strip on them at the same time; cast off; draw a string through the holes to tie behind, and one down the front to tie below the chin.

LXXXIV.—NEAT BABY'S BOOTS.

Cast on fifty-four stitches with white; wires No. 16.

Knit six rows of one stitch pearl and one plain for a top; then knit any pretty pattern for the leg, until you have it about three inches long. The following is a pretty pattern:—

First Row.

1 O X 1 O X 1 O X 1 O X, so on to the end of the row.

Second Row.
Pearl.

Third Row.
Same as the first.

When long enough, tie on the blue wool; knit two plain rows; then knit a row of holes just O X O X the whole row; knit another plain row, then knit twenty stitches, and then tie on the white; knit fourteen stitches of white; turn your work and knit three more rows of white, only knitting the fourteen stitches; tie on the blue, knit four rows; tie on the white, knit four rows; tie on the blue, knit four rows; tie on the white, knit four rows; all this time observe you are only to knit the fourteen stitches. You will now have three strips of white and two of the blue; you will now tie on the blue, and knit twenty rows;

cast off when you have the right side towards you; take up the side of what you have knitted, until you come to the stitches on the wire; you will now require three wires; join the boot at the heel, and knit along the other side until you come to the side of the strips; take up the stitches along to the toe, then knit back and forward on both wires, and knit within eight stitches of the toe the first row; the second time you come to the toe leave only seven, and so on, going one stitch nearer to the toe every time until you are quite out to the end; then knit ten rows, and finish by joining the sole together, knitting the two wires at once and casting off at the same time; sew the toe close and up the back of the leg; draw in a ribbon in the row of holes at the ankle, and make a little tuft in the instep. It requires six skeins of white Berlin and eight of blue.

LXXXV.—SHORT PURSE.

Four wires No. 18; two skeins of purse twist will be required.

Cast on two stitches on three of the wires; knit a plain round betwixt each pattern row.

First Round.

0 1 0 1 on each wire.

Second Round.

0 1 1 0 1 1 on each wire.

Third Round.

0 1 1 1 0 1 1 1 on each wire; so on until you have got twenty-six stitches on each wire; you will see that there is an O at the beginning and middle of each wire, and all the rest plain, which makes an additional plain stitch betwixt each O.

When you have twenty-six on, you then O X at the beginning and middle, the next row O X O X, so on increasing an O X at every beginning and middle until they are all O X, which continue to the end of the purse.

LXXXVI.—SIMPLE PATTERN FOR A LONG PURSE.

Cast on seventy-one stitches; knit a plain row.

First Row.
S O X O X O X to the end of the row.

Second Row.
Pearl.

Third Row.
S O X O X O X to the end of the row.

Fourth Row.
Pearl.

Fifth Row.
Pearl.

Sixth Row.
Plain.

Commence again at the first row.

It requires three skeins of purse twist, at sixpence per skein, and two wires No. 18; when done, stretch it and sew up one third at each end.

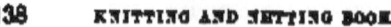

LXXXVII.—LEAF PATTERN FOR A PINCUSHION.

Knit five plain at each side for a border.

First Row.

B B B, O 1, B B B, X, 1 1 1, 1 1, X B B B.
Betwixt each row knit a back row, knitting all the pearls plain.

Second Row.

B B B, 1 0 1 0 1, B B B, X 1 1 1 X B B B.

Third Row.

B B B, 1 1 0 1 0 1 1 D D D X 1 X B B B.

Fourth Row.

B B B, 1 1 1 0 1 0 1 1 1 B B B, S X B B B.

Fifth Row.

B B B, X 1 1 1, 1 1, X B B B 0 1 0 B B B.

Sixth Row.

B B B X 1 1 1 X B B B, 1 0 1 0 1 B B B.

Seventh Row.
BBBX1XBBB,1101011BBB.

Eighth Row.
BBB§XBBB111010111BBB.

LXXXVIII.—LADY'S CRAVAT.

Pins No. 2, one ounce of white double Berlin, and one ounce of stone colour, will be required.

Cast on 100 stitches with the stone colour; knit a pearl and a plain row alternately, but take your stitch of the pin the back way, that is, put your pin in at the back of the stitch, so that it will have a twist when knitted; do so both in knitting the pearl row as well as the plain one. When you have knitted nine rows of the stone colour, take the white and knit nine rows of it; let the last row of the stone be a plain row, and the first row of the white a plain one also, so that it may appear fluted; so on until you have four strips of the stone colour, and three of the white knitted; cast off; add tassels to match, and a slide.

LXXXIX.—WARM SOLE TO WEAR INSIDE THE SHOE.

Two wires No. 10, and one ounce of six-ply fleecy wool will be required.
Cast on eighteen stitches.
Slip the first stitch the pearl way; put the thread back; knit a plain stitch; bring the thread forward; slip a stitch the pearl way; put the thread

back; knit a plain stitch; so on until the row is done; every row the same; when the length of the foot, cast off, and baste it on a piece of buckram the shape of the sole of your shoe; this makes a most comfortable sole for the winter.

XC.—BABY'S SPENCER.

Pins No. 8, a skein and half of eight-ply Lady Betty wool, half an ounce of the finest merino for the frills, and four skeins of scarlet Berlin to edge them, will be required.

Cast on eighty stitches; knit a plain row, then one row X O X O X; you then knit eighteen plain rows; you now knit only twenty-three of the stitches for one front, leaving the remainder on the pin. When you have knitted twenty-eight plain rows, you break off your thread, and tie it on for the commencement of the back, leaving the front you have knitted on the pin; you knit thirty-four for the back; when you have knitted twenty-eight rows, you again break off your thread and tie it on for the other front; when having knitted twenty-eight rows for it also, you knit all the three together, casting up two stitches at each open for the shoulder. When you have knitted two rows, you commence taking in at each side of the two stitches which were cast on; you knit three stitches past them, and turn, and knit three past the other shoulder in the same way, only taking in as you pass the last shoulder, and knitting three nearer to the front every time, until you have knitted all the stitches; you then knit a row of holes the same as the waist; then knit a plain row and cast off.

SLEEVE.

Cast on twenty-four stitches; knit nine rows of one stitch pearl, and one plain, all the rest plain, increasing a stitch at each end of every seventh row, by knitting your first and last stitch twice. When you have thirty-eight stitches on, you cast three off at the beginning of every row, until all are cast off.

FRILLS.

Take up the stitches at the neck, and knit a row of 1 0 1 0 1 0; next row plain, then five rows of X O X O X; knit a plain row betwixt each; take your scarlet wool at the last row of holes, and cast off after knitting the plain row.

You take up the stitches at the waist, and knit a frill the same; and also take up the stitches at each front with scarlet, and just cast off as soon as taken up, merely to have a scarlet edge. You knit a frill to the sleeves also, only making it four holes broad instead of six; sew in the sleeves and draw a ribbon in at the neck and waist.

XCI.—POLKA FOR A CHILD.

Pins No. 7; five skeins four-ply fleecy wool, and one skein of scarlet to edge it with, will be required.

Cast on 135 stitches with the scarlet; knit three plain rows; take the white and commence the following stitch:—Slip one the pearl way; cast up, and knit two together, the same stitch throughout the whole; knit two finger-lengths, take the scarlet and knit three plain rows; the first one you knit all the double stitches together without casting up, which will reduce your number to ninety stitches. After the three rows are knitted, make a row of holes, by casting up and taking two; you then knit other two plain rows; take your white and commence the stitch again; knit half a finger-length, then knit twenty-four stitches only for one front, a finger-length deep; knit the forty-two middle stitches a finger-length deep also for the back, then the remaining twenty-four for the other front; join the three parts together by knitting all the row; you then knit three stitches past the arm hole towards the front, then turn and knit three past the other arm hole in the same way, and every row you knit three stitches nearer to the front, until all are knitted. You then tie on your scarlet and knit three plain rows; the first you knit, take the double stitch together, but do not cast up, the same as at the waist, then a row of holes and two plain rows; you then take your white and the first row; you cast up and take the stitch single to let it out for the collar, then the other rows as usual; you knit your collar half a finger-length in depth, then put in your scarlet and take up the stitches at the end of the collar, and down each front, and knit three plain rows, then cast off.

SLEEVES.

Cast on forty-five stitches; knit three plain rows of scarlet; take the white and commence the stitch; knit two finger-lengths and a half, then cast off three at the beginning of each row, until you bring it to a point; sew up the sleeves and put them in; turn up a cuff; draw a ribbon in at the waist and neck.

XCII.—SIMPLE PATTERN FOR A COLLAR.

Wires No. 18; Smith's linen thread, No. 30.

Cast on thirteen stitches.

First Row.

8 1 1 1 0 X 1 1 0 X 1 1 1.

Second Row.

1 1 1 1, 0 X 1 1 0 X 1 1.

Third Row.

8 1 1 1 0 X 1 1 0 X 1 1 0 0 1.

Fourth Row.

1 1 B, 1 1 1 1, 0 X 1 1 0 X 1 1.

Fifth Row.

8 1 1 1, 0 X 1 1 0 X 1 1, 1 1 1.

KNITTING AND NETTING BOOK. 149

Sixth Row.
1 1 1, 1 1 1, 1 1, O X 1 1, O X 1 1.

Seventh Row.
8 1 1 1, O X 1 1, O X 1 1, O O X O O X.

Eighth Row.
1 1 B, 1 1 B, 1 1 1 1, O X 1 1 O X 1 1.

Ninth Row.
8 1 1 1, O X 1 1, O X 1 1, 1 1 1, 1 1 1, 1 1.

Tenth Row
1 1 1, 1 1 1, 1 1 1, 1 O X 1 1, O X 1 1.

Eleventh Row.
8 1 1 1, O X 1 1, O X 1 1, O O X, O O X, O O X

Twelfth Row.
1 1 B, 1 1 B, 1 1 B, 1 1 1 1, O X 1 1, O X 1 1.

Thirteenth Row.

S 1 1 1, O X 1 1, O X 1 1, 1 1 1, 1 1 1, 1 1 1.

Fourteenth Row.

Cast off three stitches, 1 1 1, 1 1 1, 1 1 1, O X 1 1, O X 1 1.

Fifteenth Row.

S 1 1 1, O X 1 1, O X 1 1, O O X, O O X, O O X.

Sixteenth Row.

1 1 B, 1 1 B, 1 1 B, 1 1 1 1, O X 1 1, O X 1 1.

Seventeenth Row.

S 1 1 1, O X 1 1, O X 1 1, 1 1 1, 1 1 1, 1 1 1.

Eighteenth Row.

Thirteen plain, O X 1 1, O X 1 1.

Nineteenth Row.
S 1 1 1, O X 1 1, O X 1 1, O O X, O O X, O O X, O O X, O O X.

Twentieth Row.
1 1 B, 1 1 B, 1 1 B, 1 1 B, 1 1 B, 1 1 1 1, O X 1 1, O X 1 1.

Twenty-First Row.
S 1 1 1, O X 1 1, O X 1 1, plain 17.

Twenty-Second Row.
Cast off three stitches, fifteen plain, O X 1 1, O X 1 1.

Twenty-Third Row.
S 1 1 1, O X 1 1, O X 1 1, then O O X to the end.

Twenty-Fourth Row.
1 1 B seven times, then 1 1 1 1, O X 1 1, O X 1 1.

Twenty-Fifth Row.

8 1 1 1, O X 1 1, O X 1 1, then twenty plain.

Twenty-Sixth Row.

Cast off four stitches, seventeen plain, then O X 1 1, O X 1 1.

Twenty-Seventh Row.

8 1 1 1, O X 1 1, O X 1 1, then O O X to the end.

Twenty-Eighth Row.

1 1 B seven times, then 1 1 1 1, O X 1 1, O X 1 1.

Twenty-Ninth Row.

8 1 1 1, O X 1 1, O X 1 1, twenty-three plain.

Thirtieth Row.

Cast off seven stitches, seventeen plain, then O X 1 1, O X 1 1; repeat the last four rows until you have thirty points; you then make the end correspond, by casting off more stitches at each point.

XCIII.—VERY PRETTY LACE COLLAR.

Wires No. 20; Smith's linen thread No. 00.

Cast on thirty-three stitches; knit a plain row.

First Row.

1 1 1, then O O X to the end.

Second Row.

1 1 B to the end.

Repeat these two rows three times, to make four holes.

Ninth Row.

1 1 1, then X X to the end.

Tenth Row.

Cast off twelve stitches, then X X to the end. When you should have thirty-three stitches on, commence again at the first row.

XCIV.—COLLAR, DIAMOND PATTERN.

Wires No. 22; Smith's linen thread No. 70.

Cast on forty-five stitches; a plain row betwixt each pattern row.

First Row.

8 1 1 O X 1 1 1, then O X 1 1 1, 1 1 1 to the end of the row.

Second Row.

8 1 1 O X 1 1, then O X O X 1 1 1 1 to the end.

Third Row.
S 1 1 O X 1, then O X O X O X 1 1 to the end.

Fourth Row.
S 1 1 O X, then O X to the end.

Fifth Row.
Same as the third row.

Sixth Row.
Same as the second row.

Commence again at the first row, and knit two pattern rows the same; the last row of the diamond and the first being the same, always knit your stitch at the beginning of the plain rows, so as to widen the edge, and slip it at the pattern rows to tighten the neck; knit an edge of the following pattern, and sew round it:—

EDGING.

Cast on fifteen stitches; knit two plain rows.

First Row.

1 1 0 X 1, O X, O X, O X, O X O O X.

Second Row.

1 1 B, 1 1 1, 1 1 1, 1 1 1, 1 1 0 X 1.

Third Row.

S 1 1 O X, 1 1 1, 1 1 1, 1 1 1, 1 1 1.

Fourth Row.

Cast off four stitches, then 1 X; cast off one on the left hand wire, then O O O O X, O O X 1, O X 1.

Fifth Row.

S 1 1 O X 1 B, 1 1 B, 1 B, 1 1 1.

Sixth Row.

1 1 1, 1 1 1, 1 1 1, 1 1 1, O X 1.
Commence again at the first row.

XCV.—POINT LACE COLLAR.

Wires No. 22; Smith's linen thread No. 70.
Cast on thirty-one stitches; knit a plain row.

First Row.
1 1 1, then O O X to the end.

Second Row.
1 1 B to the end.

Third Row
Same as the first row.

Fourth Row.
Same as the second row.

Fifth Row.
Plain.

Sixth Row.
Plain.

Seventh Row.
Plain.

Eighth Row.
Cast off seven stitches, then X X to the end.

You will now have thirty-one stitches on; commence again at the first row, so on until your collar is as large as you wish it.

XCVI.—BEAUTIFUL POINT LACE COLLAR.

Wires No. 20; Smith's linen thread No. 30.
Cast on 110 stitches very slackly; knit two plain rows.

First Row.
X O O X O O to the end of the row.

Second Row.
1 1 B, 1 1 B to the end.

Third Row.
X O X O X O to the end.

Fourth Row.
1 1 B, 1 1 B to the end.

Fifth Row.
X O X O to the end.

Sixth Row.
Plain.

Seventh Row.
X O X O to the end.

Eighth Row.
Plain.

Ninth Row.
Plain.

Tenth Row.
X X X X to the end.

Commence again at the first row; repeat the pattern five times, then work the first and second rows, and cast off very slackly.

XCVII.—SHELL PATTERN FOR A COLLAR.

Wires No. 22; linen thread No. 70.
Cast on 503 stitches; knit eight plain rows.

First Row.

S 1 1 1, 1 1 1, O 1, O 1, O 1, O 1, O 1 O. Repeat to the end; S is for the edge stitch

Second Row.

S 1 1 1, 1 1, B̽, B B B, B B B, B B B, B̽. Repeat.

Third Row.

S 1 1 1, 1 1 X, 1 1 1, 1 1 1, 1 X. Repeat.

Fourth Row.

S 1 1 1, 1 1, B̽, B B B, B B, B̽. Repeat.

Commence again at the first row, and when you

have half an inch knitted, take in a stitch at the plain part, so on taking in a stitch every half-inch, until you have all the plain stitches taken in; you then knit six plain rows and cast off; knit an edging of the following pattern, and sew round it:—

BEE'S WING EDGING.

Cast on thirteen stitches; knit a plain row.

First Row.

8, 1 O X, 1 O X, O X, O X, O 1 1.

Second Row.

Plain eleven, then O X 1.

Third Row.

8, 1 O X, 1 1, O X, O X, O X O 1 1.

Fourth Row.

Plain twelve, then O X 1.

Fifth Row.
S 1 O X, 1 1 1, O X, O X, O X, O 1 1.

Sixth Row.
Plain thirteen, then O X 1.

Seventh Row.
S, 1 O X, 1 1 1 1, O X, O X, O X, O 1 1.

Eighth Row.
Plain fourteen, then O X 1.

Ninth Row.
S, 1 O X, 1 1 1, 1 1, O X, O X, O X, O 1 1.

Tenth Row.
Plain fifteen, then O X 1.

Eleventh Row.
S, 1 O X, 1 1 1, 1 1 1, then draw over the stitches

on the left hand wire, until you have seven drawn over, which is all on the wire, you then O O 1.

Twelfth Row.
1 1 B, 1 1 1, 1 1 1, 1, O X 1.
Commence again at the first row.

XCVIII.—HANDSOME NETTED TIPPET.

A medium size mesh, and one twice the breadth; one ounce of white Derlin wool, and one of shaded purple, will be required.

Cast on seventy-five loops with the purple wool and broad mesh; you net two rows with the white wool, and narrow mesh betwixt every broad row; let out in the broad row, by putting two loops into one, every ten loops for ten rows; when you have it about forty broad rows in depth, take a very broad mesh, and put two loops into every other loop, end with two white rows with the narrow mesh.

You now net two rows of white at the neck, then put two loops into every other loop, to let out for the collar, which net same as the tippet, until you have it six rows deep, then finish to correspond with the edge; draw a ribbon in at the neck; add a few bows down the front.

––•+✠+•––

XCIX.—LONG NETTED WINDOW CURTAINS
FOR A DRAWING-ROOM.

One and a half pounds of Dutch twist No. 8, and two meshes, one an inch broad, and the other one third of an inch, will be required.

Cast on 300 loops with the narrow mesh; net sixteen rows, then one row with the broad mesh, then another row with the broad mesh, taking three loops into one, then three rows with the narrow mesh; you then net three rows with the broad mesh in the same manner as the three former broad rows; you then commence again with the sixteen rows and narrow mesh, so on until you have five broad strips.

FOR THE BORDER.

You net four loops into every other loop with the broad mesh, then take a mesh half the width of the narrow one, and net two rows, then finish with the narrow mesh, netting one loop into every other loop.

G.—WARM CUFF.

Two wires No. 10, and eight shades of brown Berlin; three skeins of each will be required.

Cast on eighty stitches with the darkest; knit three plain rows, then a row of holes by knitting X O X O X, so on throughout the whole cuff; alternately three plain rows and a row of holes, always changing your shade at every row of holes.

You dispose your shades as follows:—From the darkest to the brightest, then from the light up to the dark, so on from the dark again to the light, up to the dark again; you will have two darks, and two lights, when sewn together; cast off at the dark, and sew the two sides together, then the two ends so as they may be double.

CL—SOFA CUSHION.

You require five pins No. 9, without nobs at the end, and twelve shades of green, purple, and amber Berlin.

Cast on five stitches on each of four of the pins; a plain row is knitted betwixt each pattern row; you cast up a stitch, two from each end of every pin, until you have seventeen stitches on each pin. You now commence your pattern, but continue casting up a stitch, two stitches from each end throughout the whole cushion. Your pattern is:—1 1 0 edge, then 1 0 1 0 1 1 1 X X 1 1 0 1 0 1, end 0 1 1, every pattern row the same; but you will observe you have only one plain stitch betwixt your end stitches and the pattern; every row they will increase one, and when you have eleven plain, you can make another pattern at each side of the first pattern, so on as your cushion enlarges.

In working the pattern, you will observe to put your O over the O, and the X over the X in the former row. You change your shade every pattern row, only knitting two rows of each shade; when you have all your shades in, cast off.

Dispose your shades in the following manner:—Commence with light green; after the darkest green, take the darkest purple, and after the lightest purple, take the lightest amber, ending with dark amber. When made up, a button is sewed in the centre, and drawn down.

CIL.—SHETLAND HANDKERCHIEF
SAME PATTERN AS A SOFA CUSHION.

Commence at the centre of the neck; of course

you only require two pins; every other row is a pearl row.

First Row.
1 1 0, edge stitches 1 1 1 1, edge 0 1 1.

Second Row.
1 1 0, edge stitches 1 0 1 1 1 1 0 1, edge 0 1 1.

Third Row.
1 1 0, edge stitches 1 1 1 0 1 1 1 0 1 1 1, edge 0 1 1.

Fourth Row.
1 1 0, edge stitches 1 1 1, 1 1, 0 1 1 1 1 0, 1 1 1, 1 1, edge 0 1 1.

Fifth Row.
1 1 0, edge stitches 1 1 1, 1 1 1, 1 0 1 1 1 1 0, 1 1 1, 1 1 1, 1, edge 0 1 1.

Sixth Row.
1 1 0, edge stitches 1 1 1, 1 1 1, 1 1 1, 0 1 1 1 0, 1 1 1, 1 1 1, 1 1 1, edge 0 1 1.

Seventh Row.
1 1 0, edge stitches 1 1 1, 1 1 1, 1 1 1, 1 1, 0 1 1 1 0, 1 1 1, 1 1 1, 1 1 1, 1 1, edge 0 1 1.

Eighth Row.
1 1 0, edge stitches 1 0 1 0 1 1 1, X X, 1 1, 0 1 0 1 0 1 1 1 1 0 1 0 1 0 1 1 1 X X 1 1 0 1 0 1 0 1, edge 0 1 1.

You continue repeating the eighth row, but observe that you place the O over the O, and the X over the X. In the former row, your edge and middle are always the same. In the eighth row you have only one plain stitch betwixt your edge and the pattern, also only one on each side of the middle; they will increase every row, and when you have eleven plain, you can begin another pattern on each side of the first.

CIII.—VICTORINE.

You require two shades of grey double Berlin, and two pins No. 10.

You knit with both shades at a time; cast on twenty-four stitches; it is all plain knitting, only you make a loop row every other row, by passing one of your threads round your finger before knitting the stitch; put both threads round the pin in the usual manner to knit a plain stitch; your other row you knit plain, but always knitting with double threads; one row of loops you make with the darkest, and the next row you make with the lightest, so on changing every row.

When you have half a yard knitted, you commence to shape the neck, which you do by making a stitch at the end of every plain row, until you have another finger-length knitted; you now take in a stitch at the commencement of every row, still continuing to increase a stitch at the end of the row. After knitting about another finger-length, taking in at the beginning, and increasing at the end, you then take in, and let out every other plain row five times; you then knit a finger-length without either letting out or taking in, and then cast off, which is the one half of the Victorine; you knit the other half in the same manner, only with this difference: you increase at the beginning, and take in at the end of the row; you sew it together, taking as deep a seam as to make the loops meet; line it with silk.

CIV.—NETTED VICTORINE.
GREEN AND SCARLET.

It requires three shades of green, and four of scarlet; two skeins of each of the scarlets; five of the darkest green, and four of each of the other shades, and four skeins of white for the edge.

Cast on 100 loops on a mesh an inch and quarter broad, with the darkest green; double; take a mesh a quarter of an inch broad, and work two rows of the dark green, but single; then work two rows of the lightest green, and then two rows of the middle shade.

You now take the darkest scarlet, and work one row with double wool on a mesh half an inch broad, second shade next, double also, but take two loops together, then a row of the third shade, double also, putting two stitches into every loop.

You now take the smallest mesh, and net two rows with the darkest green, two of the second shade, two of the third shade, then two rows of the lightest scarlet.

You now take a mesh an inch broad, and the white wool; put six loops into every third stitch; next row you take the smallest mesh, and put one stitch into every loop with the darkest green; another row of the next shade to finish.

You now take up the loops and work the other side to correspond from the broad double row.

DIRECTIONS FOR WASHING.

SHETLAND WORK.

Wash in lukewarm water and boiled soap; put a little blue in the water; do not rub, but squeeze it, and press the water out without wringing; you then pin it out on a sheet on the floor, and iron it, putting paper betwixt the iron and the work; put it through thin starch.

FLEECY WORK.

Wash in the same manner as the Shetland; you then shake it before the fire until nearly dry, then spread it out into a proper shape.

EDINBURGH: PRINTED BY T. NELSON AND SONS.

PART II.

CROCHET WORK

TO THE RIGHT HONOURABLE

LADY AUGUSTA GORDON LENNOX

THIS VOLUME OF

Useful and Ornamental Crochet Work,

IS, BY PERMISSION,

MOST RESPECTFULLY DEDICATED BY

The Authoress.

PREFACE.

Numerous works have already appeared, designed as Books of Reference for those desirous of acquiring the graceful and truly feminine art of Crochet Work. The following Work possesses peculiar claims to the attention of those wishing to master all the varieties of this elegant accomplishment. It will be found to contain a very complete assortment of useful articles, combined with a great variety of those which are chiefly intended to exercise the fair student's ingenuity for purposes of ornament; and not the least of its recommendations will be found in the fact, that nearly all the patterns are original, and, therefore, only to be obtained from its pages: while the utmost care has been taken to simplify the descriptions, so as to render the work an easy, popular, and comprehensive Key to the practice of this useful and elegant art. The Authoress has aimed at producing a book which shall become an essential companion of the Lady's Work Table; and, with this in view, no labour or expense has been spared to secure for it the varied fruits of ingenuity and experience.

EXPLANATION OF STITCHES.

Chain Stitch.—Draw the thread through the loop on the needle.

Single Crochet.—Keep one loop on your needle; put the needle through the upper edge of the chain, and draw the thread through the chain stitch and the loop on the needle at the same time.

Double Crochet.—Insert your needle into the upper edge of the chain stitch on the work, and draw the thread through the work; then through the two loops on the needle.

Long Crochet.—Catch the thread round the needle before you insert it into the work; draw the thread through the work, then through *one* loop, then through *two* loops, then through the *two* loops remaining on the needle.

EXPLANATION OF STITCHES.

Double Long Crochet.—Catch, or place, the thread *twice*, round the needle before you insert it into the work; then draw the thread through the work, then through one loop, and then through two loops successively, until you have drawn the thread through all the loops on the needle.

Treble Long Crochet.—The same as double long crochet, with the simple difference of the thread being put three times round the needle instead of twice.

Open Crochet.—Catch the wool round the needle before you insert the needle into the work; draw the thread through the work, then through one loop, then through two loops, again through two loops, and then through one loop.

To carry on two threads at the same time.—Place the thread you are not using over the first finger of your left hand, and when you draw the thread you are using through the work, take it below the one you are not using; and when you draw it through the loops on the needle, catch the thread up above the one over your finger. Of course, you can only carry on two threads when you work in double crochet stitch.

EXPLANATION OF STITCHES.

Round.—Is when you continue working all round any piece of work.

Row.—Is when you work back and forwards, or from end to end of your work.

Increase.—Put your needle twice into the same stitch.

Decrease.—Put your needle into two stitches at the same time, or miss a chain stitch.

Each stitch in the description of the patterns is to be repeated until the round or required length is obtained.

The words, loops and chain stitches, signify the same.

All the needles mentioned in this work are numbered by the Bell Gauge.

When choosing wools of different shades for Crochet Work, it is not so necessary that the shades be so near in resemblance with regard to colour as for knitting; the effect indeed being better when the shades are not too close.

INDEX.

I.	Very Beautiful Baby's Cap,	Page 1
II.	Beautiful Broad Lace for a Frill,	13
III.	Collar—Pine Pattern,	16
IV.	Honiton Lace Collar,	22
V.	Brussels Lace Collar,	25
VI.	Collar with an open Border,	29
VII.	Collar—Valenciennes Pattern,	33
VIII.	Collar,	39
IX.	Round Collar,	42
X.	Collar—Of a Simple Pattern,	44
XI.	Cuff,	47
XII.	Pretty Cuff,	50
XIII.	Edging,	53
XIV.	Edging,	55
XV.	Open Edging,	55
XVI.	Broad Honiton Edging,	56
XVII.	Narrow French Edging,	57
XVIII.	Narrow Brussels Edging,	58
XIX.	Edging,	59
XX.	Edging—Leaf Pattern,	61

INDEX.

XXI.	Close Edging,	Page 63
XXII.	Broad Open Edging,	ib.
XXIII.	Fine Honiton Edge,	66
XXIV.	Handsome Carriage Bag,	67
XXV.	Very Pretty D'Oyley—for Salver,	69
XXVI.	Black Silk Mitts,	77
XXVII.	Patterns for One Dozen Wine Rubbers—Pattern First,	79
XXVIII.	Second Rubber,	84
XXIX.	Third Rubber,	87
XXX.	Fourth Rubber,	90
XXXI.	Fifth Rubber,	93
XXXII.	Sixth Rubber,	95
XXXIII.	Seventh Rubber,	97
XXXIV.	Eighth Rubber,	100
XXXV.	Ninth Rubber,	102
XXXVI.	Tenth Rubber,	105
XXXVII.	Eleventh Rubber,	107
XXXVIII.	Twelfth Rubber,	109
XXXIX.	Baby's Sponser,	119
XL.	Long Scarf—Pink and Grey Stripes,	116
XLI.	Square Bag,	118
XLII.	Ear Cap,	119
XLIII.	Muffatees—With a Frill at one Edge,	121
XLIV.	Round Cushion,	122
XLV.	Turkish Sofa Cushion—Worked in Stripes,	124
XLVI.	Beautiful Cushion,	126

	INDEX.	xiii
XLVII.	Mitts of Berlin Wool,	Page 127
XLVIII.	Berlin Wool Cuff—Light and Dark Brown,	129
XLIX.	Spanish Smoking Cap,	ib.
L.	Blue Bonnet for a little Boy,	132
LI.	Cover for a Round Pincushion,	136
LII.	Chenille Bag,	137
LIII.	Ribbon for the Neck,	ib.
LIV.	Turkish Scarf for the Neck,	139
LV.	Small Handkerchief,	140
LVI.	Warm Handkerchief for the House,	142
LVII.	Scarf of Diamond Pattern,	ib.
LVIII.	Collar of Berlin Wool,	143
LIX.	Collar for a Child—Of Primrose and Pink Berlin,	146
LX.	Gaiters for a Little Boy,	148
LXI.	Lady's Slipper,	149
LXII.	Baby's Boots,	151
LXIII.	Baby's Shoe,	152
LXIV.	Jug Stand,	154
LXV.	Bird Nest Flower Stand,	156
LXVI.	Flower Stand with Frill,	158
LXVII.	Toilet Cover,	149
LXVIII.	Bonnet Cap,	161
LXIX.	Toque,	163
LXX.	Very Beautiful Turkish Tiddy,	164
LXXI.	Round Purse,	167
LXXII.	Long Purse, with Beads—Scarlet and Gold,	169

INDEX.

		Page
LXXIII.	Striped Purse,	171
LXXIV.	Short Purse,	173
LXXV.	The Star Wine Rubber,	175
LXXVI.	Large Round Stand—With a Frill,	178
LXXVII.	Chinchilla Muff,	181
LXXVIII.	Anti Macassar—Diamond Pattern,	182
LXXIX.	Anti Macassar—Wave Pattern,	187
LXXX.	Bread Basket Napkin,	193
LXXXI.	Collar—Spider Net Pattern,	196
LXXXII.	Comfortable Prudence Cap,	202
LXXXIII.	Opera Cap—Square at the Ears,	203
LXXXIV.	Elegant Opera Cap,	206
LXXXV.	Carriage Cap,	209
LXXXVI.	Lady's Polka—With an Ermine Border,	212
LXXXVII.	Child's Polka,	216
LXXXVIII.	D'Oyley—For a Salver or Bread Plate,	219
LXXXIX.	Pretty Simple Scarf—For a Child,	226
XC.	Band for the Neck,	227
XCI.	Blue Bonnet for Holding Pence,	229
XCII.	Pen Wiper,	230
XCIII.	Beautiful Under Sleeve,	231
XCIV.	Trimming,	239
XCV.	Vandyke Trimming,	241

RUBBERS.

RUBBERS.

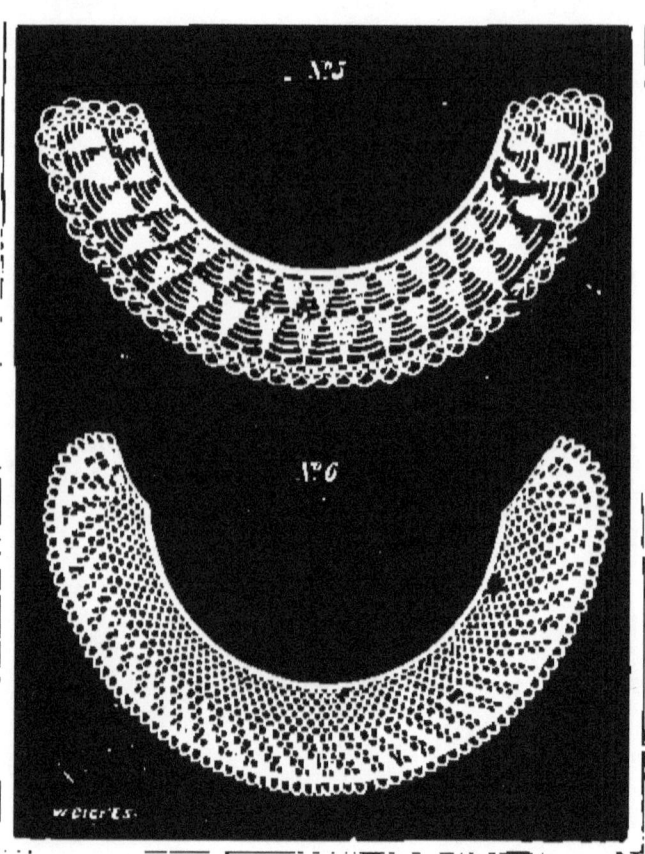

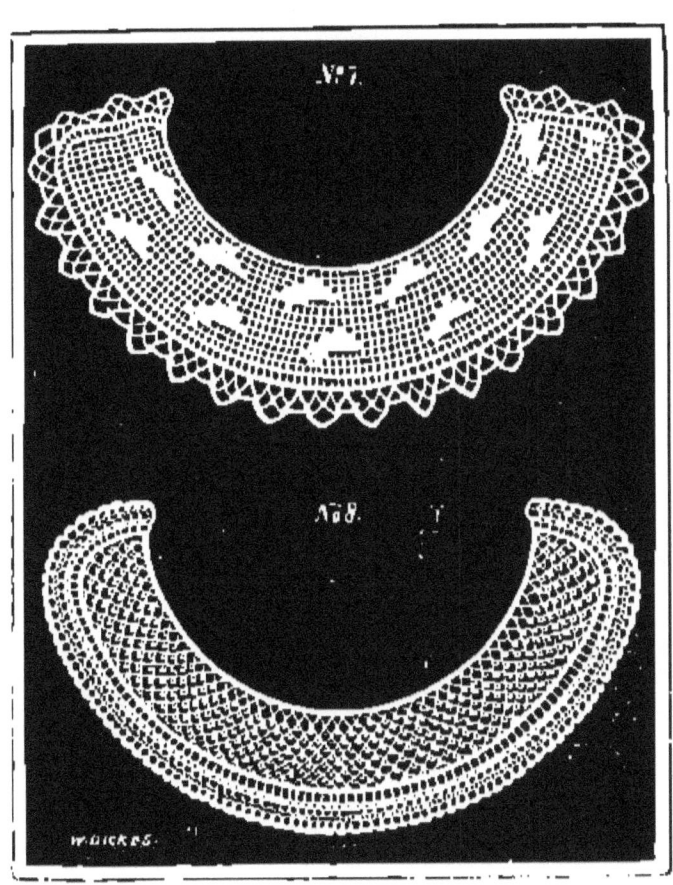

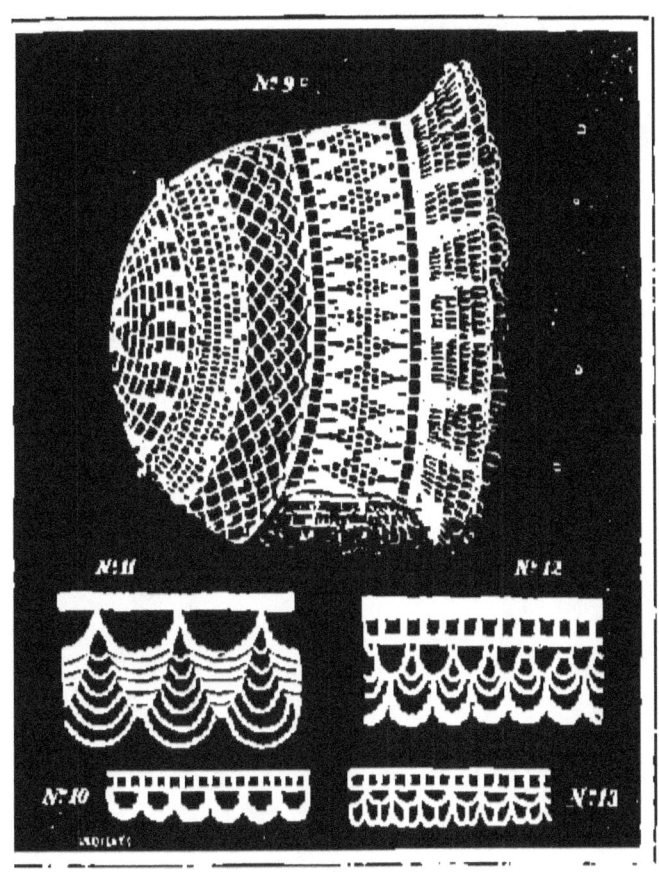

9. VERY BEAUTIFUL BABY'S CAP. PAGE L | 12. EDGING, LEAF PATTERN. PAGE 61.
10. NARROW BRUSSELS EDGING. PAGE 58. | 12. BROAD HONITON EDGING. PAGE 56.
13. NARROW FRENCH EDGING. P. 57.

CROCHET WORK.

I.—VERY BEAUTIFUL BABY'S CAP.

(See Engraving. No. 9.)

Boar's Head cotton, Nos. 30, for the cap, and 40, for the border; which is worked on to the cap. Work with a fine crochet needle.

You commence at the centre of the crown; tie a loop on the end of the thread.

First Round.
Work twelve double crochet stitches into the loop.

Second Round.
Put two long stitches into each stitch

Third Round.
Put three long stitches into three successive

stitches and make a chain of three betwixt each three long stitches.

Fourth Round.

Put two long stitches over the three in the last round, and make a chain of five betwixt each two long stitches.

Fifth Round.

Put one long stitch over the two long ones in the last round, and make a chain of five, then a long stitch in the centre of the chain in the last round, again a chain of five, and a long stitch over the two.

Sixth Round.

Put one long stitch over each long one, and one between each long stitch in the last round, making a chain of two between each stitch.

Seventh Round.

Put two long stitches above the first long stitch,

then make a chain of *two*, and put *one* long stitch above the next one in the last round, again the chain of *two*, and then the *two* long stitches.

Eighth Round.

Put *three* long stitches above the two long ones in the last round, and *one* long stitch over the one —making always a chain of *two* between the three and the one.

Ninth Round.

Put *four* long stitches above the three, and *one* above the one, in the last round, making *two* chain stitches between the one and the four.

Tenth Round.

Put *five* long stitches above the four, and *one* above the one, in the last round, always making a chain of *two* between the five and the one.

Eleventh Round.

Put *one* long stitch into every chain stitch. The crown is now finished.

MIDDLE PART.

First Round.

Put *one* long stitch into every other chain stitch on the crown, make a chain of two between each long stitch.

Second Round.

Put *one* long stitch into every open hole, making a chain of *two* between each.

Third Round.

Same as the last.

Fourth Round.

Same as the last, only putting *four* long stitches into every eighth open hole to form a spot.

Fifth Round.

Same also, only put three long stitches into two successive holes after you pass the spot in the last round.

Sixth Round.

Put six long stitches into six successive chain stitches of the last round, making two chain stitches betwixt each six, and missing two on the work.

Seventh Round.

Put three double crochet stitches above the open in the last round, and make a chain of eight betwixt each four.

Eighth Round.

Make a chain of eight, join it to the fourth stitch on the chain in the last round, then make a chain of four, and join it to the next stitch on the chain, which will form a small loop; you then make a chain of eight again, joining it to the centre of the next chain, making the little loop in the same manner.

Ninth, Tenth, Eleventh, and Twelfth Rounds.
Same as the seventh.

Thirteenth Round.
Put four double crochet stitches into the centre of the chain in the last round, and make a chain of three betwixt each four.

Fourteenth Round.
Put six long stitches into six successive chain stitches, commence them in the last two of the four double crochet stitches in the last round, and work them across the chain part, making a chain of one betwixt each six, and missing one chain stitch on the work betwixt each six.

The middle part is now done; you break off the thread and commence the front part; you must

CROCHET WORK.　　　　7

break off your thread at the end of every row, and begin again always at the same end; when you finish the row, work the thread down a stitch or two to fasten; and in commencing the row, tie the thread on to the end that was left hanging when you began the former row, which will prevent you having so many ends.

FRONT PART.

First Row.

Make a long open row for a caser, put the thread three times round the needle for the long stitch, and put one long stitch into every open, and one in the centre of the six close stitches in the last row, making a chain of three betwixt each; you leave four inches for the neck.

Second Row.

Put three long stitches into the open in the

last row, and one chain stitch betwixt each three.

Third Row.

Put seven long stitches into seven successive chain stitches on the last row, making two chains betwixt each seven

Fourth Row

Put five long stitches in the centre of the seven in the last row, and one into the open, making a chain of two between the one and the five long stitches.

Fifth Row.

Put three long stitches in the centre of the five in the last row, and put one into each of the open holes, with a chain of two betwixt each single stitch, and the three also.

Sixth Row.

Put one long stitch into the centre of the three

in the last row, and one into each hole, always making a chain of two betwixt each long stitch.

Seventh Row.

Put three long stitches into the three chain stitches opposite the point, and one long stitch into the two holes, making a chain of two betwixt each one and the three.

Eighth Row.

Put five long stitches above the three in the last row, of course one will come on each side, and put one into the open with the two chains betwixt as formerly.

Ninth Row.

Put seven long stitches above the five, with one on each side of the five, and make a chain of two betwixt each seven.

Tenth Row.

Put three long stitches into the first three long

stitches in the last row, make a chain of one, then three long stitches again.

Eleventh Row.

Make a caser the same as the other one, put one long stitch into every open, and make three chain stitches betwixt each long stitch.

Twelfth Row.

Put one long stitch into every chain stitch.

BORDER PART.

You now commence the border with No. 40 cotton; you work all round for the first border, then put a double one at the front, which is worked the same stitch, but work it into the chain stitches at the back of the last row on the cap close to the caser.

First Round.

Put one long stitch into every chain stitch,

making three chain stitches betwixt each; In working the long stitches on the border, put the thread twice round the needle to make it more open.

Second Round.
Same as the last, but put the long stitch into every open.

Third Round.
Same as the last.

Fourth Round.
Make a chain of five, and join it with a double crochet stitch, to the chain opposite the long stitch in the last round.

Fifth Round.
Put three double crochet stitches into the three centre stitches of the chain in the last round, making a chain of three betwixt each three double stitches.

You now put two rows round the crown to give it a finish.

First Round.

Make a chain of six, and join it to the fourth chain stitch at the edge of the last round of the crown; again a chain of six.

Second Round.

Make a chain of six, and join it to the centre of the chain in the former round by two double crochet stitches; make it up according to taste.

II.—BEAUTIFUL BROAD LACE FOR A FRILL

Boar's Head cotton, No. 36. Work with a very fine needle.

Make a chain a yard long; you break off your thread at the end of every row; when you com-

CROCHET WORK. 13

mence again, tie on the thread at the end that was left hanging when you began the former row; next row you must leave an end, then the next again tie on the thread to prevent so many ends being left.

First Row.
Double crochet.

Second Row.
Make a chain of eight and join it to every fifth chain stitch with a double crochet stitch.

Third Row.
Make a chain of eight, join it to the fourth stitch of the chain in the last row, then make a chain of four, and join it to the next chain stitch, then, again, a chain of eight, joining it to the fourth stitch of the chain in the former row.

Fourth, Fifth, Sixth, and Seventh Rows.
Same as the third.

Eighth Row.

Make a chain of five, and join it to the centre of the chain in the former row with two double crochet stitches.

Ninth Row.

Put five long stitches into the open betwixt the two double crochet stitches in the last row, making a chain of two betwixt each five.

Tenth Row.

Put two long crochet stitches into the open betwixt the five long stitches in the last row, making a chain of four betwixt each two long stitches, and two chain stitches betwixt the two long ones.

Eleventh Row.

Put five long stitches betwixt each two long stitches in the last row, and make one chain stitch betwixt each long stitch.

Twelfth Row.

Make a chain of eight, and join it to the last row, with one double crochet stitch betwixt each five long stitches in the last row.

Thirteenth Row.

Make six double crochet stitches on the chain in the last row; of course you leave one at each end, as there was eight in the chain; make a chain of two betwixt each six.

Fourteenth Row.

Make four double crochet stitches in the six double crochet stitches in the last row, and a chain of four betwixt each four.

Fifteenth Row.

Make two double crochet stitches in the centre of the four in the last row, with a chain of six betwixt each two.

Sixteenth Row.

Make two double crochet stitches above the two in the last row, with a chain of eight betwixt each two double crochet stitches.

When washed and dressed, draw it up, and baste it on a ribbon.

III.—COLLAR.
PINE PATTERN.
(See Engraving, No. 3.)

Boar's Head cotton, No. 24.

Make a chain fifteen inches long. In working this pattern, you must break off your thread at the end of every row, and commence always at the other end; fasten your ends in the same manner as described in working the broad lace.

First Row.

Long crochet into every chain stitch.

Second Row.

Make a chain of five, and join them to the last row in the fourth chain stitch with one long crochet stitch, another chain of five, joining them with two double crochet stitches on the next fourth and fifth chain stitches, again a chain of five, joining every alternate five with a long stitch. You begin and end all the rows with the chain stitches, and tie on the thread in the third stitch.

Third Row.

Make a chain of four, then put nine long stitches into nine successive chain stitches, four on each side of the long stitch, always making four chain stitches betwixt each nine long ones.

Fourth Row.

Make a chain of eight, then put seven long stitches on the seven chain stitches in the middle of the nine long stitches in the last row, and make a chain of six betwixt each seven.

Fifth Row.

Make a chain of ten, then make five long stitches over the seven in the last row, and a chain of eight betwixt each five.

Sixth Row.

Make a chain of twelve, then put three long stitches over the five in the last row, making a chain of ten betwixt each three.

Seventh Row.

Make a chain of nine, then one long stitch into the centre of the last chain, then a chain of six, and put one long stitch into the centre of the three in the last row, again one long stitch into the centre of the chain, making always six chain stitches betwixt each long stitch.

Eighth Row.

Make a chain of six, then put eleven long

stitches into eleven successive chain stitches, commencing one chain stitch from the point of the last pine, and make four chain stitches betwixt each eleven long stitches.

Ninth Row.

Make a chain of eight, then put nine long stitches over the eleven, commencing one from the end, and always make a chain of six betwixt each nine long stitches.

Tenth Row.

Make a chain of ten, then put seven long stitches over the nine in the last row, with a chain of nine betwixt each nine long stitches.

Eleventh Row.

Make a chain of twelve, then put five long stitches over the seven long stitches in the last row, with a chain of eleven betwixt each five long stitches.

Twelfth Row.

Make a chain of fifteen, then put three long stitches above the three centre stitches of the five in the last row, making a chain of thirteen betwixt each three long stitches.

Thirteenth Row.

Make a chain of ten, then one long stitch in the centre of the chain in the last row, then a chain of eight, and one long stitch in the centre of the three long stitches in the last row, the next long stitch is put in the centre of the chain, make eight chain stitches betwixt each long stitch.

You now commence

THE BORDER;

Tie the thread on at the neck.

First Row:

Put three long stitches into the open betwixt

each row in working down the ends, and make two chain stitches betwixt each three, after you pass the end the opens will be longer, so put six long stitches into each, but always make a chain of two betwixt each three.

Second Row.

Put two double crochet stitches into the first open betwixt the three in the last row, then make a chain of three, and put two long stitches into the next open, with one chain stitch betwixt the two long ones, again a chain of four, and two double crochet stitches into the next open, then the chain of three and the two long stitches.

Third Row.

Put three double crochet stitches above the two long stitches in the last row, and make a chain of six between each three double crochet stitches, in passing round the corner, put a few more stitches into the chain to make it lie flat.

IV.—HONITON LACE COLLAR.

Boar's head cotton, No. 30. Use a fine steel crochet needle.

Make a chain twelve inches long.

First Row.

Long crochet, that is, catch the thread round the needle, put the needle into every chain stitch, draw the thread through, then through two loops, again through two loops.

Second Row.

Open crochet, making two chain stitches betwixt every long stitch, and missing only one stitch on the work.

Third Row.

Open crotchet, but put your stitch into every large hole, and make two chain stitches betwixt each.

Fourth Row.

Open crochet, but put four stitches into every sixth hole, and make no chain stitches betwixt the four, but the two chain stitches betwixt all the others.

Fifth Row.

Open crochet, putting four stitches in the hole, on each side of the one, where there were four stitches put in the last row.

Sixth Row.

Open crochet, putting four stitches into the hole that comes betwixt the four close stitches in the last row.

Seventh Row.

Open crochet, putting one stitch in the centre of the four close ones.

Eighth Row.
Open crochet.

Ninth Row.

Same as the first, but take your thread and commence at the end of the first row, and work round each end; in the former rows you work backwards and forwards, and never bring off your thread.

You now commence the border, which consists of three rows.

First Row.

Put four long stitches into every fifth chain stitch, and put one chain stitch betwixt each long stitch

Second Row.
Put five long stitches, same as the last, into each stitch, that is, betwixt the four in the last row.

Third Row.
Same as the last.

V.—BRUSSELS LACE COLLAR.
(See Engraving, No. 5.)

Boar's head cotton, No. 14.
Make a chain ten inches long.

First Row.
Close long crochet.

Second Row.
Make a chain of five, join it to the last row on every third chain stitch, with a double crochet stitch, again five chain stitches, joining them to the work every third stitch

Third Row.

Make a chain of five loops and join them by a double crochet stitch to the centre stitch of the chain in the last row.

Fourth, Fifth, Sixth, Seventh, and Eigth Rows.

Are done in the same manner as the third.

You now break off your thread and join it at the neck part, so as to work round each end.

THE BORDER.
First Row.

Put five long stitches into the end of the first row at the neck, make a chain of three, then a long stitch into the centre of the hole, then a chain of three, five long stitches into the next hole, a chain of three, then the single long stitch, again the chain of three, and then five long stitches into the next hole.

You break off your thread at the end of every

row, and commence always at the same end in working the border.

Second Row.

In this row you put six long stitches together, and commence the long stitches at the centre of the five stitches in the last row, you then make a chain of three, then put a single long stitch into the first of the next five close long stitches, again a chain of three, and then the six long stitches.

Third Row.

You now make seven long stitches close together, putting the first of the seven on the centre of the six in the last row, then the chain of three, and again the single long stitch at the commencement of the next six close stitches in last row.

Fourth Row.

You now make eight long stitches close together,

commencing them as in the two former rows, at the centre of the close stitches in the last row, then a chain of three, and the single long stitch in the same manner also.

Fifth Row.

You make nine long stitches close together, commencing them as in the former rows, and working the chain and single stitch in the same manner also.

Sixth Row.

You work this row all the long stitch close together, that is, put your needle into every chain stitch.

Seventh Row.

You make a chain of six, and join it to the work on the fifth and sixth chain stitches, by two double crochet stitches.

VI.—COLLAR, WITH AN OPEN BORDER.

Boar's head cotton, No. 24.
Make a chain 14 inches long.

First Row.

Long crochet into every chain stitch.

Second Row.

You make this row one inch in from each end, every row after you work back and forward, without breaking off the thread, until you come to the border, you must then break off your thread and commence at the neck, on the inch that was left, you then work back and forward again.

MANNER OF WORKING SECOND ROW.

Make two long stitches close together, then a chain of two, then one long stitch into the second chain stitch from the two long stitches; again a chain of two, then the two long stitches close together, into the second chain stitch from the one long stitch.

Third Row.

Make three long stitches over the two in the former row, and one long stitch over the one, always making two chain stitches betwixt the close long stitches and the single long stitch.

Fourth Row.

Make four long stitches over the three in the former row, and one over the one, and two chain stitches betwixt the close stitches and the single one.

Fifth Row.

Same as the last, only putting five long stitches over the four in the last row.

Sixth Row.

Same as the last, but put six long stitches over the five in the former row.

Seventh Row.

Same as the last, only putting seven long stitches over the six in the last row.

Eighth Row.

Same as the last, but put eight stitches over the seven in the last row. You now commence

THE BORDER.

First Row.

Join your thread on to the inch that was left, two chain stitches from the middle, make a chain of three, then one long stitch, a chain of four, then two long stitches with one chain stitch betwixt them; again a chain of four, and one single long stitch; when you come to the corner you put the single long stitch into the centre of the close stitches, and the two long stitches over the two open parts.

Second Row.

Put one long stitch on each side of the single long stitch in the former row, with one chain stitch betwixt them, and put one long stitch betwixt the two in the last row, with a chain of five betwixt each long stitch.

Third Row.

Same as the last, only making a chain of six instead of five betwixt the single stitches and the two long ones; and when you pass the corner you must make some additional chain stitches, to make the work lie flat.

Fourth Row.

Put six long stitches into every large hole,

make them close together, and make two chain stitches betwixt each six long stitches.

Fifth Row.

Put two long stitches into the hole, and make a chain of seven betwixt each two.

VII.—COLLAR.
VALENCIENNES PATTERN.
(See Engraving, No. 7.)

Boar's Head cotton, No. 36. Work with a very fine needle.

Make a chain twelve inches long.

First Row.

Long crochet into every chain stitch.

Second Row.

Long crochet, with a chain of two betwixt each stitch, and put your stitch into every other chain stitch in the work.

Third Row.

Put one long stitch immediately over the long stitch in the last row, after having done eight stitches you put three long stitches close together.

Fourth Row.

Put one long stitch over every long stitch in the last row, but when you come to the three together, you put three long stitches into the hole before the three, and put one into every chain over the three till you come to the other side, when you put three again into the next hole. You then continue your one stitch over the one in the last row, with two chain stitches betwixt each, until you come to the next three close stitches; you work across them in the same manner as the last.

Fifth Row.

You work this row same as the last, putting

CROCHET WORK.

three into the hole before and after the close stitches, and one into every chain stitch over them, with one long stitch over every single long stitch.

Sixth Row.

You put three long stitches into the hole before the close stitches, and seven stitches, one into every chain stitch, which makes ten close together: you then put one stitch into every other chain, with two chain stitches betwixt each until you are past the close part; you then put one over the one in the last row, as in the former rows.

Seventh Row.

You work this row same as the last, but only make three close stitches, which you put in the centre of the close ones in the last row.

Eighth Row.

Put one long stitch over every long one, and

put a chain of two betwixt each long stitch. There are not any close together in this row.

Ninth Row.

Same as the third row, but put the three stitches that are together opposite the point of the last spot.

Tenth Row.

Same as the fourth row.

Eleventh Row.

Same as the fifth.

Twelfth Row.

Same as the sixth.

Thirteenth Row.

Same as the seventh.

Fourteenth Row.

Same as the eighth.

You now commence
THE BORDER,
and work round each end.

First Row.
Tie your thread on at the neck, and put three long stitches into each hole, and make one chain stitch betwixt each three long stitches.

Second Row.
Put one long stitch into the open betwixt each three in the last row, and make a chain of two betwixt each long stitch.

Third Row.
Put three long stitches into each hole, and make one chain stitch betwixt each three long stitches.

Fourth Row.
Make a chain of eight and join it to the work by two double crochet stitches betwixt each six stitches in the last row.

Fifth Row.

Work double crochet up to the centre of the chain stitches in the last row, then make a chain of eight; join it by two double crochet stitches to the centre of the next chain, again a chain of eight; join them to the centre of the next chain, and work double crochet into every chain stitch until you come up to the centre of the next chain, then make your eight chain stitches again.

Sixth Row.

Make a chain of five from each point of the thick work, then work double crochet up to the centre of the chain in the last row. You now make a chain of nine and join it to the centre of the next chain, work double crochet down to the point of the thick work in the last row.

CROCHET WORK.

Seventh Row.
A double crochet stitch into every chain stitch.

VIII.—COLLAR.

Boar's Head cotton, No. 24.
Make a chain fourteen inches long.
First Row.
Long crochet into every chain stitch.
Second Row.
You leave an inch and a half at each end, to attach the border to; put two long stitches into two successive chain stitches, and make two chain stitches betwixt each two, and miss one chain on the work between each two.
Third Row.
Put two long stitches into the hole betwixt the

two close stitches in the last row, and make two chain stitches betwixt each two.

Fourth Row.
Same as the last.

Fifth Row.
Put only one long stitch into each hole, and make a chain of four betwixt each stitch.

Sixth Row.
Put three long stitches into each open, and make a chain of two betwixt each three.

Seventh Row.
Same as fifth.

Eighth Row.
Same as sixth.

Ninth Row.
You now commence working round for the ends Tie your thread on at the part that was left at the

neck of the collar, and attach every row to it; make a chain of five, and join it to the work on the last row by two double crochet stitches, in the open betwixt the three close stitches.

Tenth Row.

Make a chain of six, and join it to the centre of the chain in the last row with a double crochet stitch.

Eleventh Row.

Put six long stitches into the chain in the last row, and make one chain stitch between each six.

Twelfth Row.

Put four long stitches into the open betwixt each six close stitches in the last row, and make one chain stitch between each long stitch.

Last Row.

Put five long stitches into the open between

each four long stitches in the last row, and make one chain betwixt each long stitch.

IX.—ROUND COLLAR.

Boar's Head cotton, No. 24.
Make a chain fourteen inches long.

First Row.
Long open crochet into every chain stitch.

Second Row.
Put two long stitches into two successive chain stitches on the work, and make a chain of two between each two long stitches, and miss one chain stitch on the work. This row you commence two inches in from each end of the work, and every row after you attach to the piece that was left, which will form the collar round at the ends.

Third Row.

Put two long stitches into the open betwixt the two in the last row, and make a chain of two between each two long stitches.

Fourth Row.

Same as the last.

Fifth Row.

Same as the last, only make a chain of three instead of two.

Sixth Row.

Same as the last.

Seventh Row.

Same as the two last.

Eighth Row.

Double crochet into every chain stitch.

Ninth Row.

Make a chain of six, and attach it to the work on every fourth and fifth chain stitch by two double crochet stitches.

Tenth Row.

Same as the last, attaching the chain to the two centre stitches of the chain in the last row.

Eleventh Row.

Same as the last.

Twelfth Row.

Put four long stitches into the four centre stitches of the chain in the last row, and make a chain of three between each four.

Last Row.

Put five long stitches into the open in the last row, and make one chain stitch between each long stitch.

X.—COLLAR,

OF A SIMPLE PATTERN.

Dour's Head cotton, No. 20.
Make a chain fifteen inches long.

First Row.
Long crochet into every chain stitch.

Second Row.
Commence this row two inches in from each end. Put two long stitches into two successive chain stitches, miss two chain stitches on the work between each two, and make a chain of three betwixt each two long stitches.

Third Row.
Put two long stitches into each open, and make three chain stitches betwixt each two long stitches.

Fourth, Fifth, and Sixth Rows.
The same as the third.

Seventh Row.
Break off your thread and tie it on at the neck, and work round each end every row until finished, then join each row to the piece that was left at the ends. This row you put a long stitch into every chain stitch.

Eighth Row.
Long crochet, making three chain stitches betwixt each long stitch, and missing two chain stitches on the work.

Ninth Row.
Long crochet into every chain stitch.

Tenth Row.
Put four long stitches into one chain stitch, and

make one chain stitch betwixt each long stitch; then put another four into one chain stitch; again missing four chain stitches on the work.

Eleventh Row.

Put four long stitches into the chain stitch between the four long stitches in the last row.

Work other three rows in the same manner as the eleventh, which complete the collar.

XI.—CUFF.

Boar's Head cotton, No. 22.
Make a chain six inches long.

First Row.

Long crochet into every chain stitch.

Second Row.

Make a chain of six stitches, join it to the work by two double crochet stitches on every fourth and fifth chain stitch.

Third Row.

Make a chain of six, and join it to the centre of the chain in the last row with two double crochet stitches.

Fourth Row.

Same as the last.

Fifth Row.

Make a chain of four, join it, as in the last row, to the centre of the chains in the former rows.

Sixth Row.

You now commence to work round each end. Put five long stitches in every other large hole, and make a chain of five betwixt each five long stitches.

Seventh Row.

Put five long stitches into each hole, and a single long stitch into the centre of the five close ones in the last row; make a chain of two betwixt the single long stitch and the five close stitches.

Eighth Row.

Put a long stitch into every other chain stitch on the work, and make one chain stitch betwixt each long one.

Ninth Row.

Same as the last.

Tenth Row.

Make a chain of six, and join it into every other stitch in the last row

Eleventh Row.

Put four long stitches into every chain stitch

in the last row, and make one chain betwixt each four long stitches.

Twelfth Row.

Put two long stitches into the hole betwixt the four close stitches in the last row, and make a chain of four betwixt each two long stitches.

XII.—PRETTY CUFF.

Fine Boar's Head cotton. Work with a fine steel needle.

Make a chain five inches long; work one row of long open crochet. You work all round afterwards.

First Round.

Long open crochet; and put four stitches into each end hole.

Second Round.
Double crochet.

Third Round.
Open crochet; into every chain stitch, (instead of every other one in turning the ends,) to make it lie flat.

Fourth Round.
Open crochet; but in turning the ends put two stitches into each hole.

Fifth Round.
Double crochet.

Sixth Round.
Make a chain of eight loops; attach it to the former round on every fifth stitch; work three double crochet stitches.

Seventh Round.

Work four stitches of open crochet into the four centre stitches of the chain in the former round; then make a chain of two loops.

When worn, draw a narrow ribbon through the centre row.

XIII.—EDGINGS.
Open Edging.

Fine Boar's Head cotton. Work with a fine steel crochet needle.

Make a chain the length required in working edging. Break off the thread and commence every row at the right hand.

First Row.

Make a chain of seven loops, join it to the fifth

stitch on the chain; then work three double crochet stitches.

Second Row.
Make a chain of seven loops, join it to the three centre stitches of the chain in the last row.

Third Row.
Another row the same as the second. Finish with a row of double crochet.

XIV.—EDGING.

Make a chain as long as your piece of edging is required.

First Row.
Make three long crochet stitches into three stitches on the chain, make a chain of three loops,

and then the three long stitches, missing three stitches on the chain.

Second Row.
Same as the last, only observe to make the three long stitches opposite the large hole.

Third Row.
Make a chain of six loops, join it to the fifth stitch, and work two double crochet stitches.

Fourth Row
Put two open crochet stitches into the third and fourth chain stitches on the last row; and make two chain stitches.

XV.—OPEN EDGING.

Make your chain as long as required.

First Row.
Make a chain of seven loops, join it to every fourth chain stitch.

Second Row.
Same as the last row, but join the chain to the middle stitch of the chain in the last row.

Third Row.
Make a chain of seven loops, join it to the centre stitch on the chain in the former row, then work seven double crochet stitches.

XVI.—BROAD HONITON EDGING.

Bóar's Head cotton, No. 24.
Make a chain as long as required.

First Row.
Long crochet into every chain stitch.

Second Row.
One long and two chain stitches; missing two on the work.

Third Row
Double crochet.

Fourth Row.
Eight chain and two double crochet stitches, missing four stitches on the work.

CROCHET WORK. 57

Fifth Row.
Six double crochet into the chain; then four chain.

Sixth Row.
Four double crochet above the six; then six chain.

Seventh Row.
Two double crochet stitches above the four; then eight chain.

Eighth Round.
Double crochet.

XVII.—NARROW FRENCH EDGING.

(See Engraving, No. 12.)

Boar's Head cotton, No. 22.
Make a chain as long as required.

First Row.

Open crochet—that is, one long, one chain, miss a chain.

Second Row.

Two double crochet, then seven chain, missing three chain stitches.

Third Row.

Two double crochet stitches above the two in the last row, five chain, one double crochet into the centre of the seven chain, then five chain.

XVIII.—NARROW BRUSSELS EDGING.

(See Engraving, No. 16.)

Make a chain as long as you wish.

First Row.

Put one long stitch into every other chain

stitch, and make one chain stitch between each long stitch.

Second Row.

Make a chain of six, and join it to the work on every fourth and fifth chain stitch with two double crochet stitches.

Last Row.

Double crochet into every chain stitch,

XIX.—EDGING.

Make a chain as long as you wish.

First Row.

Double crochet.

Second Row.

Make a chain of five loops; join it to the work on every fourth stitch.

Third Row.

Put five long stitches into every fourth hole, make one chain stitch at the beginning and end of the five, then a double crochet stitch into the centre stitch of the next chain in the last row; then a chain of five, and join it to the centre stitch in the former row; again a chain of five. After it is joined, make one chain stitch, then the five long stitches.

Fourth Row.

Make a chain of five, join it to the centre of the chain in the last row, again a chain of five, and join it to the centre of the close stitches.

Last Row.

Double crochet into every chain stitch.

XX.—EDGING.

LEAF PATTERN.
(See Engraving, No. 11.)

Boar's Head cotton, No. 30.
Make a chain as long as you require.

First Row.
One long stitch into every other stitch, one chain between each.

Second Row.
Fourteen chains, two double crochet into the ninth and tenth chain stitches.

Third Row.
Twelve double crochet stitches into the chain, leaving one at each end; then four chain.

Fourth Row.
Ten double crochet above the twelve; then six chain.

Fifth Row.

Eight double crochet above the ten; then seven chain stitches.

Sixth Row.

Six double crochet above the eight; then eight chain stitches.

Seventh Row.

Four double crochet above the six; then ten chain stitches.

Eighth Row.

Two double crochet above the four; then twelve chain stitches.

XXI.—CLOSE EDGING.

Make a chain the length you wish

First Row.

Long crochet into every chain stitch.

Second Row.

Put five long stitches into the sixth chain stitch, and make one chain stitch, between each long stitch.

Last Row.

Put five long stitches between each five on the last row, and make one chain between each long stitch.

―――✠―――

XXII.—BROAD OPEN EDGING.

Make your chain as long as you require your piece of edging.

First Row.

Long crochet into every other chain stitch, and make one chain stitch between each long stitch.

Second Row.

Make a chain of six, and attach it to the work on every fourth and fifth chain stitch, with two double crochet stitches.

Third Row.

Make a chain of six, and attach it to the two centre stitches of the chain in the last row.

Fourth Row.

Same as the third.

Fifth Row.

Make a chain of six, and join it to the centre of the chain in the last row by two double crochet stitches; you again make a chain of six, and after joining it to the centre of the chain in the last row, work double crochet up to the centre of the next chain.

Last Row.

From the centre of the chain next the double crochet stitches, you work four double crochet stitches, which will bring you down to the double stitches in the last row, then make a chain of three across to the other side of the double stitches, you then double crochet up to the centre of the chain, then make a chain of six, which join to the centre of the chain.

XXIII.—FINE HONITON EDGE.

Boar's Head cotton, No. 30. Work with a fine steel needle.
Make a chain as long as you require.

First Row.

A long stitch into every other chain stitch, with one chain betwixt each stitch.

Second Row.

Put one long stitch into every other open stitch, and make three chain stitches between each long stitch.

Third Row.

Put four long stitches into every other hole, and make a chain of three between each three long stitches.

Fourth Row.

Make a chain of nine stitches, and join it to the centre of the four close stitches in the last row, with a double crochet stitch.

Last Row.

Double crochet into every chain stitch, except the chain stitch over the double crochet stitch in the last row,—being in the corner it would not lie flat if a stitch was put into it.

XXIV.—HANDSOME CARRIAGE BAG.

It will require two and a half ounces of shaded double Berlin:—green, scarlet, purple, blue, and amber, half an ounce of each. Commence with green.

Make a chain of ninety-six loops.

First Row.

Three long stitches, three chain, repeat, missing three chains. Afterwards work round each side with scarlet, putting the three long stitches into the openings between the three green long stitches.

Every round the same, changing the colour at the commencement of each, and use them in the order named.

When you have repeated the colours five times, it will be large enough.

Line it with black silk. Either add a clasp or draw in a narrow piece of whalebone at the top; let it be about a third shorter than the bag, so as it may hang a little full; add cord for strings.

XXV.—VERY PRETTY D'OYLEY,

FOR SALVER.

Boar's Head cotton, No. 12.

Tie a loop and work twenty-four long stitches into it, large enough to pass a pencil through.

First Round.

Put one long stitch into every other chain stitch, and make four chain stitches betwixt each long stitch.

Second Round.

Put two long stitches into the chain stitch above the long stitch in the last round, making a chain of four betwixt each two long stitches.

Third Round.

Put three long stitches above the two in the last

round, putting two into the second stitch, making a chain of four betwixt each three long stitches.

Fourth Round.

Put four long stitches above the three in the last round, putting the two last into the same stitch, making a chain of four betwixt each four long stitches.

Fifth Round.

Same as the last, only putting five above the four. The chain of four the same.

Sixth Round.

Put six above the five, with the chain of four betwixt each.

Seventh Round.

Put seven above the six, then the chain of four betwixt each seven.

Eighth Round.

Put eight above the seven, and the chain of four between each eight.

Ninth Round.

Put nine above the eight, and the chain of four betwixt each nine.

Tenth Round.

Put ten above the nine in the last round, with the four chain stitches betwixt each ten.

Eleventh Round.

Put nine long stitches above the ten, (you now leave off putting two into the last stitch,) make a chain of five betwixt each nine.

Twelfth Round.

Put eight above the nine, then make a chain of

three, and put a long stitch into the middle stitch of the chain in the last round, then three chain stitches, and again the eight long stitches.

Thirteenth Round.

Make seven long stitches over the eight, then a chain of three, and a long stitch into the centre stitch of the two chains in the last round, making a chain of three betwixt each long stitch and the seven long stitches.

Fourteenth Round.

Put six long stitches over the seven, and one long stitch into the centre of the chain in the last round, with the chain of three betwixt each single long stitch, and also the six long stitches; you have now three single long stitches.

Fifteenth Round.

Put five over the six long stitches in the last

round, and the single long stitches and chain in the same manner as the last; you will have four single stitches in this round.

Sixteenth Round.

You put four over the five long stitches in the last round, and make the single long stitches and the chain in the same manner; you now have five single stitches.

Seventeenth Round.

Put three above the four, and the single stitches and chain in the same manner; you will now have six single long stitches in this round.

Eighteenth Round.

Put two long stitches above the three; work the single stitches and the chain in the same manner as the former rounds.

Nineteenth Round.

This round is all single long stitches, with a chain of three betwixt each. Observe always to put a stitch above the two in the last round, and one in the centre of the chain of three.

Twentieth Round.

Put one long stitch in the centre of the chain in the last round, and a chain of three betwixt each stitch.

Twenty-first Round.

Put three long stitches into the three chain stitches of the last round, and make one chain stitch betwixt each three long stitches.

Twenty-second Round.

Make a chain of five, and join it into every open

betwixt the three long stitches in the last round with a double crochet stitch.

Twenty-third Round.

Put three double crochet stitches in the centre of the five chain stitches of the last round, and make a chain of five betwixt each three long stitches.

Twenty-fourth Round.

Put a double crochet stitch into the centre of the chain of five, and make a chain of three betwixt each double crochet stitch.

Twenty-fifth Round.

Put three long stitches into the three chain stitches of the last round, and make one chain stitch betwixt each three long stitches

Twenty-sixth Round.

Make a chain of six, and join it into every

open betwixt each three with a double crochet stitch.

Twenty-seventh Round.

Make a chain of six, and join it to the two centre stitches of the chain in the last round with two double crochet stitches.

Twenty-eighth Round.

Put four double crochet stitches into the four middle stitches of the chain in the last round, and make a chain of four betwixt each four double crochet stitches.

Last Round.

Put two double crochet stitches, in the middle of the four double stitches in the last round, and make a chain of six betwixt each two double crochet stitches.

XXVI.—BLACK SILK MITTS.

It will require three-quarters of an ounce of stout sewing silk, and a fine steel needle.

Make a chain of eighty loops, or as many as you will require to go over the hand.

Work three rounds of double crochet, then an open round; again three rounds of double crochet.

You now continue to work in open crochet, but commence letting out for the thumb, by putting two stitches into one, which will be the top of the gusset; every alternate round afterwards you increase on each side of the last increase.

When you have as much worked as will bring you to the thumb, you commence it by working a chain of four loops, and joining it to the fifteenth open stitch from where you make your chain, and let it be the part that was let out.

Work six open rounds, then three rounds of double crochet; you finish by working a chain of five loops, and joining it to every third stitch.

You now tie your silk on at the bottom of the thumb and work round the hand; continue for seven open rounds, then three rounds of double crochet; you now work a chain of five loops, join them to every third stitch, another round of a chain of five, joining them to the centre of the chain in the last round.

You now work two rounds of the chain stitch at the top, to correspond with the bottom.

Draw a ribbon in the open round at the top, and darn in some of the holes on the back to form a pattern.

XXVII.—PATTERNS FOR ONE DOZEN WINE RUDDERS.

(See Engraving, No. 1.)
First.

Boar's Head cotton, No. 10.

Tie a loop large enough to pass a pencil through, and work twelve double crochet stitches into it.

First Round.

Put two long stitches into every other chain stitch, and make a chain of two betwixt each two long stitches.

In joining the rounds, draw the thread through the first stitch of the round and the one on the needle, and work a chain of three to raise the thread up for the next round.

Second Round.

Put three long stitches above the two in the last round, put the two last into the same stitch, and make a chain of two, betwixt each three long stitches.

Third Round.

Put four long stitches above the three in the last round, the two last into the same stitch, and make a chain of three betwixt each four long stitches.

Fourth Round.

Put five long stitches above the four in the same manner, and the chain of three betwixt each five long stitches.

Fifth Round.

Put six long stitches above the five, and the chain same as in the last round.

Sixth Round.

Put seven above the six chain the same as in last round.

Seventh Round.

You now leave off putting two into the last long stitch; put six long stitches above the seven and make a chain of four betwixt each six long stitches.

Eighth Round.

Put five long stitches over the six, and put one long stitch into the open where the chain is in the last round, and make three chain stitches betwixt the five long stitches and the single long one.

Ninth Round.

Put four long stitches above the five; one into each of the two opens, with a chain of three betwixt the single stitches and the four long stitches.

Tenth Round.

Put three long stitches above the four, and a single one into each open, with the chain as in last round.

Eleventh Round.

Put one single long stitch into each open, and one above the three, with a chain of three betwixt each long stitch.

Twelfth Round.

Put a long stitch into each chain stitch.

You are now at the border, which consists of four rounds. The same border is made to all the wine rubbers.

THE BORDER.

First Round.

Put seven double crochet, then seven chain, missing three stitches on the work.

Second Round.

Put five double crochet stitches over the seven double crochet stitches in the last round, then five chain, and one double crochet stitch into the centre of the chain of seven, then five chain stitches.

Third Round.

Put three double crochet stitches into the centre of the five double crochet stitches, then five chain, one double crochet stitch into the fourth stitch of the chain, then four chain, one double crochet into the second stitch of the next chain, then five chain stitches.

Fourth Round.

All double crochet, but miss the last and the first stitch of the scollop; one double crochet betwixt the two that are missed.

XXVIII.—SECOND WINE RUBBER.

Tie a loop and work in double crochet, letting out on the first round on every stitch, and afterwards, let out every second stitch; when you have thirty-four stitches round, you commence the pattern.

First Round.

One long stitch into every chain stitch, and make one chain stitch betwixt each long stitch.

Second Round.

Put two long stitches into one stitch, make a chain of two, put one long stitch into the second stitch from the two, then a chain of two.

Third Round.

Put one long stitch over the single long one in

CROCHET WORK.   85

the last round; make a chain of two, put three long stitches above the two long stitches, (put two into the first stitch, and one into each of the next two chain stitches,) then the chain of two.

Fourth Round.

Same as the last, putting four above the three close ones, always putting two into the first one,—the one above the single long stitch, and the chain of two,—betwixt the close stitches and the single long stitch.

Fifth Round.

Same as the last, only putting five above the four close stitches.

Sixth Round.

Same as the last, only putting six above the five.

Seventh Round.

Put one long stitch into each open, and one in the centre of the close stitches, with a chain of three betwixt each long stitch.

Eighth Round.

A long stitch into every open, with a chain of three betwixt each long stitch.

Ninth Round.

A long stitch into every chain stitch, and no chain between.

Border, same as the first.

XXIX.—THIRD WINE RUBBER.

Tie a loop, and work twelve double crochet stitches into it.

First Round.

Put one long stitch into each chain stitch, and make two chain stitches betwixt each long stitch.

Second Round:

A long stitch into every chain stitch, and two into every second one to increase it.

Third Round.

Put one long stitch into every chain stitch, and make three chain stitches betwixt each seven long stitches, which will make it into eight divisions.

Fourth Round.

Put five long stitches above the five middle stitches of the seven close ones in the last round; make a chain of three, then one long stitch into the open; again a chain of three.

Fifth Round.

Put three above the three middle close stitches a chain of three, a long stitch into the open; a chain of three, a long stitch into the next open, a chain of three.

Sixth Round.

Put one long stitch above the three, and a long one into every open, with a chain of three betwixt each.

Seventh Round.

Put one long stitch into every open, with a chain of three betwixt, but put three long stitches, close together, above the single long stitch betwixt each point.

Eighth Round.

One long stitch into every open, and five close together above the three in the last round; make a chain of three betwixt each single long stitch.

Ninth Round.

One long stitch into every open, with the chain of three between, and put three close long stitches in the middle of the five in the last round.

Tenth Round.

A long stitch into every open, and one in the

centre of the three close ones, with a chain of three betwixt each.

Eleventh Round.

A long stitch into every chain stitch.
Border, same as the first.

XXIX.—FOURTH WINE RUBBER.

Tie a loop, work twelve double crochet stitches into it.

First Round.

Put two long stitches into every chain stitch.

Second Round.

Put three long stitches into every other chain

stitch, and make a chain of two betwixt each three long stitches.

Third Round.

Put five long stitches above the three close stitches; put two into the first chain stitch, and pass the three one stitch, so as the five is even above; make a chain of two betwixt five long stitches.

Fourth Round.

Put seven long stitches above the five in the same manner as the last round, with a chain of two betwixt each seven.

Fifth Round.

Same as the last, but put nine above the seven, and one long stitch into the open.

Sixth Round.

Put seven long stitches in the seven middle

stitches of the nine, and one stitch into each open, with a chain of two between each single stitch.

Seventh Round.

Put five stitches above the seven, one into each open; a chain of two betwixt each single one.

Eighth Round.

Three above the five, one into each open, with the chain of two betwixt each single long stitch.

Ninth Round.

One into each open, and one in the centre of the three, with the chain of two between each long stitch.

Tenth Round.

A long stitch into each chain stitch.

XXXI.—FIFTH RUBBER.

Make a chain of three, join them, and work round, putting two stitches into each until you have twenty-two stitches in the round.

First Round.

Put one long stitch into every chain stitch, and make two chains between each long stitch.

Second Round.

Put two long stitches into the chain stitch above the first long stitch, a chain of two, a long stitch above the next long stitch, then a chain of two.

Third Round.

Put three stitches above the two, put the two

last into the same chain stitch, a chain of two, a long stitch, then a chain of two.

Fourth Round.
Same as the last, but put four above the three.

Fifth Round.
Same as last, but put five above the four.

Sixth Round.
Same, but put six above the five.

Seventh Round.
Same, but put seven above the six.

Eighth Round.
Same, but put eight above the seven.

Ninth Round.
One stitch into every chain stitch.

XXXII.—SIXTH RUDDER.
(See Engraving, No. 1.)

Tie your loop, and work fifteen double crochet stitches into it.

First Round.
Put two long stitches into every chain stitch.

Second Round.
Put five long stitches, into five successive stitches, a chain of three betwixt each five long stitches.

Third Round.
Put three long stitches in the centre of the five in the last round, a chain of three, one long, a chain of three, one long, then a chain of three.

Fourth Round.

Put one long into each open, and one in the centre of the three long stitches, with a chain of three betwixt each long stitch.

Fifth Round.

One long stitch into every chain stitch.

Sixth Round.

Put one long stitch into every chain stitch but make a chain of three betwixt each seven long stitches.

Seventh Round.

Put five long stitches above the seven long stitches, one long one into the open, a chain of three between the one and the five.

Eighth Round.

Put three long stitches above the five long

stitches one into each open, three chains between the single ones and the three.

Ninth Round.

Put one long stitch into each open, and one in the centre of the three, with a chain of three betwixt each stitch.

Tenth Round.

One long stitch into every chain stitch.

XXXIII.—SEVENTH RUDDER.

Tie your loop, and work sixteen double crochet stitches into it.

First Round.

Two long stitches into every chain stitch.

Second Round.
Make six chain, and put one double crochet into the third and fourth chain on the foundation.

Third Round.
Make seven long stitches into each open, and three chain stitches between each seven.

Fourth Round.
Put three double crochet stitches into the chain of three in the last round, with a chain of eight betwixt each three.

Fifth Round.
Put nine long into the chain of the last round, with four chain between each nine.

Sixth Round.
Put seven long stitches above the nine, then

three chain, one long, three chain, one long, and three chain.

Seventh Round.

Put five long stitches above the seven, then one long one into each open, with a chain of three between the five and each one.

Eighth Round.

Put three long stitches above the five, then one into every open, and three chain stitches betwixt each.

Ninth Round.

Put one long stitch into every open, and one above the three, and three chain between each.

Tenth Round.

One long stitch into every chain stitch.

XXXIV.—EIGHTH RUBBER.

Tie a loop, work twelve double crochet stitches into it, continue working in double crochet, increasing on every second stitch until you have eight stitches.

First Round.

Put seven long stitches into seven chain stitches, make a chain of two, miss one chain stitch on the work between every seven.

Second Round.

Put seven long stitches above the seven in the last round, and a chain of three between each seven.

Third Round.

Put five long stitches above the seven, make a chain of three, put one stitch above the open, and a chain of three.

Fourth Round.

Put three long stitches above the five, then a chain of two, one long stitch above the open, a chain of two, a long stitch above the single one in last round, a chain of two, and a long stitch above the open.

Fifth Round.

Put a long stitch in the centre of the three, one above the open, then one above all the single stitches, with a chain of two betwixt each.

Sixth Round.

Double crochet.

Seventh Round.

Put two long stitches into two chain stitches, then a chain of four, and miss three chains on the work.

Eighth Round.

A long stitch into every chain stitch.

XXXV.—NINTH RUBBER.

Tie a loop, and work eighteen double crochet stitches into it.

First Round.

Two long stitches into each chain stitch.

Second Round.

Put one long stitch into every other stitch, make two chain between each long.

Third Round.

Make four long stitches, then three chain, one long into the open, three chain, one long, and three chain.

Fourth Round.

Put ten long stitches above the four in the last round, three will come on each side, then three chain stitches, one long into the open, and three chain.

Fifth Round.

Put ten long stitches above the ten in the last round, then three chain, and one long into each open, with three chain between.

Sixth Round.

Put four long in the centre of the ten, then three chain, one long into each open, and three chain between each.

Seventh Round.

Put two long into each open, then two chain stitches between each two, and two long above the four.

Eighth Round.

Put three long stitches above the two, and two chain stitches between each three.

Ninth Round.

One long stitch into each stitch.

XXXVI.—TENTH BUBBER.
(See Engraving, No. 3.)

Tie a loop, work eighteen double crochet stitches into it.

First Round.
Two long stitches into each chain stitch.

Second Round.
Make six chain stitches, then one double crochet into the fourth stitch.

Third Round.
Put eight long stitches into the chain, and two chains between each eight.

Fourth Round.
Put seven long stitches above the eight, then two chain, one long into the open, and two chain.

Fifth Round.

Put six long stitches above the seven, and one long stitch into each open, and two chain stitches between each, and the six long stitches.

Sixth Round.

Put five long stitches above the six, one long into each open, and two chain stitches between the six, and the single ones.

Seventh Round.

Put four long stitches above the five, then two chain stitches, one long into each open, and two chain stitches between each.

Eighth Round.

Put three long stitches above the four, then two chain stitches, one long into each open, and two chain stitches between each.

Ninth Round.

Put one long stitch above the three, two chain stitches, one long into each open, with a chain of two between each long stitch.

Tenth Round.

One long stitch into each chain stitch.

XXXVII.—ELEVENTH RUBBER.

Tie a loop, work eighteen double crochet stitches into it.

First Round.

Two long stitches into each chain stitch.

Second Round.

Two long stitches into each chain stitch.

Third Round.

Put one long stitch into every other stitch, and two chain stitches between each.

Fourth Round.

One long into every stitch, increasing one every six stitches.

Fifth Round.

Make seven long stitches, then two chain stitches, miss two.

Sixth Round.

Put five long stitches above the seven, make two chain stitches, one long stitch into the open and two chain stitches.

Seventh Round.

Make three long stitches in the centre of the five, two chain, one long stitch into each open, two chain between.

Eighth Round.

Put one long stitch in the centre of the three, and one into each open, with a chain of two between each long stitch.

Ninth Round.

One long stitch into each chain stitch.

XXXVIII.—TWELFTH RUBBER.
(See Engraving, No. 4.)

Tie a loop, and work fifteen double crochet stitches into it.

First Round.

Put two long stitches into each chain stitch, and one chain stitch between each two long stitches

Second Round.
Make four chain stitches, then one double crochet stitch into the open between each two.

Third Round.
Put four long stitches into the four chain stitches, and one chain stitch between each four.

Fourth Round.
Make six chain stitches, then one double crochet stitch into the open betwixt the four long stitches in the last round.

Fifth Round.
Make seven long stitches into the chain, then make two chain stitches.

Sixth Round.
Make eight chain stitches, then one double crochet stitch into the open between the seven.

Seventh Round.

Put seven long stitches into the chain, make two chain stitches.

Eighth Round.

Put five long stitches above the seven, make two chain stitches, one long into the open, then two chain stitches.

Ninth Round.

Three long stitches above the five, two chain stitches, one long into each open then two chain stitches.

Tenth Round.

Put one long stitch in the centre of the three, two chain stitches, one long stitch into each open, then two chain between each.

Eleventh Round.

One long stitch into each chain stitch.

XXXIX.—BABY'S SPENSER.

For a child about a twelvemonth old it will require two and a half ounces of shaded blue, single Berlin, and half an ounce of white to edge it. Work with a coarse ivory needle.

It is buttoned up the back.

Commence at the back with blue. Make a chain ten inches long, work in double crochet stitch, inserting the needle into the edge of the chain furthest from you, to make the work appear in ridges. In turning the rows, always make a chain stitch, to keep it straight at the edge, as you cannot put the needle into the last stitch.

Work eight ridges, (observe it takes two rows to form a ridge.) You now commence sloping for the waist and shoulders, which you do by turning your rows two stitches from each end; work other five ridges in this manner, which finishes one side of the back; work the other to correspond.

Front.

Make a chain the same length as the straight part between the two slopes, and increase two stitches every row until you have it as long as the back. You then work four ridges of the same length. You now commence sloping for the front of the neck by turning the rows at the top one stitch from the end. When you have worked four ridges in this manner, you commence sloping it up again for the other side by increasing a stitch every row at the top. Make both sides to correspond.

Before you crochet the shoulder together

work three rows of double crochet between the back and front at the shoulder, to form a little band.

Sleeve.

Make a chain eight inches long. You work back and forward from the wrist to the shoulder, slope it up to the top, then slope it down again from the middle. The sleeve must be twelve ridges wide.

Work a cuff of the same stitch; work it to the sleeve before you crochet it together; work three ridges, and then three rows of the common double crochet with the white.

Band at the Waist.

Take the white and work two rows of common double crochet, then a row of open for a ribbon, then one row of double crochet. You now take the blue and work a fall at each side, open in front; the first row you increase on every second stitch. When you have four ridges wrought, edge it with white, same as the cuff. Work the other side the same.

Collar.

In working the first row you keep it tight, as it will be rather wide, and then increase every sixth stitch on the second and third rows, to make the collar sit flat. Work four ridges, then edge it with white, same as the cuffs. The collar is worked in two parts, same as the fall at the waist. When you edge the collar, work down the back at the same time; and every two inches miss three chain stitches, and work three chain stitches, then join it to the work, which will make an open for a button hole. You do this on the first row of white. Sew in the sleeves, and draw a ribbon in at the waist.

L

XL.—LONG SCARF.

PINK AND GREY STRIPES.

It will require four ounces of pink, five ounces of grey, and one ounce of primrose, to edge the stripes. Work with a coarse needle.

You commence with pink. Make a chain three yards long. Work three rows of long crochet. You work backwards and forwards.

You now take the primrose and work one row of double crochet.

Now take the grey, and work twelve rows of open crochet. The first row you put your stitch into every other chain stitch on the primrose. The following rows you put your stitch into the open between each long stitch.

After the twelve rows of grey, you work one row of double crochet with the primrose, then you work three rows with the pink in the same manner as the last three pink rows.

You continue working pink and grey stripes alternately, edging them with the primrose, until you have three stripes of grey, and four stripes of pink. When done, you work a row of double crochet with the primrose at the edge you commenced at, to make it correspond with the othe edge.

Crochet a fringe in at each end; put grey in opposite the grey, and pink opposite the pink, and primrose at the primrose; knot the fringe.

XLI.—SQUARE BAG.

Fifteen shades of scarlet Berlin and an ivory crochet needle will be required.

Commence with the darkest shade. Make a chain of forty loops, work a row on each side of the chain of the double crochet stitch. The whole bag is done the same stitch. You work two rounds of each shade. When you have all the shades in, it will be large enough. Work the frill in the following manner:—

Take one of your middle shades, and work a round of open crochet into every chain stitch. You then change your shade, and do the same stitch all round again, with this difference: you put your needle into the large hole instead of the stitch. You work the third row in the same manner, with another shade. You finish with a round the same stitch as the bag.

You line it, and sew rings inside at the bottom of the frill.

XLII.—EAR CAP.

It will require three skeins of blue, and six skeins of white Berlin.

You make a chain of one hundred loops. You work the same stitch throughout, which is open crochet.

CROCHET WORK.

After you have the first row done you work all round, putting your needle into every large hole, and as you turn round the ends you work the stitch twice into the end holes, to make it lie flat.

You work three rounds of white, then one round of the blue, and then one of white.

Draw a blue ribbon down the centre.

XLIII.—MUFFATEES,

WITH A FRILL AT ONE EDGE.

Four skeins of scarlet, and six of white Berlin wool will be required, and an ivory needle.

Commence with scarlet. Make forty loops, work three rounds, after you join your chain, of the double crochet stitch.

You then work seven rounds of white, the open crochet stitch. You take up only every other loop in your first round, but in your other rounds you put the needle through the large hole.

When you have done the seven rounds, you tie on the scarlet, and work three rounds of double crochet stitch, the same as the beginning.

You work the frill the same as the open part, but take up every chain stitch, work two rounds of white, then finish with one round of scarlet the double stitch.

XLIV.—ROUND CUSHION.

You require two colours of shaded wool. Purple and amber make a good contrast. You work the double crochet stitch, and carry on both threads at one time.

Make three stitches of the amber, join them and work round, putting two stitches into one. You have now six: put in the purple, and work a stitch of each colour into every stitch, to enlarge it for the two first rounds. Every round afterwards you only increase by putting two stitches into the last stitch of each colour. You change your threads, and work the purple on the purple stitches, and the amber on the amber stitches. Continue working in the same manner until as large as you wish it.

Line it with velvet, and draw it down in the centre with a button.

XLV.—TURKISH SOFA CUSHION.

WORKED IN STRIPES.

You require one ounce of gold colour, and half an ounce of each of the following colours—of double Berlin, green, scarlet, blue, white, and purple. You work them in the order named, and a narrow gold strip betwixt each colour. It will be sufficiently large when you have repeated the stripes twice.

You commence with the gold colour. Make a chain half a yard in length, and work three rows of double crochet.

You now take the green and work four rows in the following manner:—Put three long stitches into three successive chain stitches in the work, then make a chain of three loops, and put your next three long stitches into the work three chain stitches distant from the last long stitches. The three following rows you put your long stitches into the large hole.

You now work three rows of double crochet with the gold colour; then take the scarlet and work in the same manner as the green.

When made up, you line the work with black velvet, and make the back of scarlet, with chenille cord and tassels.

XLVI.—BEAUTIFUL CUSHION.

It requires five colours of shaded double Berlin, half an ounce of each—green, scarlet, purple, blue, and amber. You work one row of each. Commence with green. Make a chain of one hundred and twenty loops. You put three long stitches into three successive stitches, then make a chain of three loops, again your three long stitches, missing three stitches on the chain. Every row afterwards you put the three long stitches into the large hole. Use the colours in the order named. When all are wrought up, the cushion will be sufficiently large. It is made up in the same manner as the one in the last pattern.

XLVII.—MITTS OF BERLIN WOOL.

It will require fourteen skeins of claret colour, and five of blue Berlin. Use an ivory crochet needle.

Commence with blue. Make a chain of forty-five loops, join it, and work four rounds of double crochet.

Take the claret and work in open crochet.

When you have four open rounds done, you increase by putting two stitches into one hole. You let out every other round, one on each side of the first let out, until you have twelve rounds done altogether from the blue.

You now work the thumb. Join it together at the ninth hole, and work three rows round, then work two rounds of double crochet with blue.

Work four rounds from the bottom of the thumb, and finish by working two rounds of double crochet with blue.

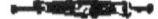

XLVIII.—BERLIN WOOL CUFF

LIGHT AND DARK BROWN

Make a chain five inches long. Work in double crochet stitch, but always insert your needle into the edge of the chain furthest from you. Work back and forward until you have as much as will go easily over the hand, then crochet it together.

You now take your light brown and work round each end until you have about two inches, which you turn up on to the dark brown.

XLIX.—SPANISH SMOKING CAP.

Half an ounce of shaded purple single Berlin,

five shades of blue greens, one skein of each shade, and six skeins of primrose, will be required.

Work with a steel crochet needle, No. 14.

Make a chain of three loops with the primrose, join them, work in double crochet stitch; put two stitches into each.

Take the purple, work one primrose and one purple into each stitch; next round work two primrose into each primrose, and two purple into each purple stitch.

Every succeeding round work one purple into each purple stitch, and one primrose stitch into each primrose one, except the last, in which you work two stitches, in order to increase it. Continue working in the same manner until you have eight primrose stitches betwixt the two purple ones.

You now work the last stitch of the primrose

with purple, and make the increase on the last purple stitch. Continue working in the same manner until you have only one primrose stitch left. You then break off your primrose, and continue working with the purple alone.

You now only increase in every other round, and do so for three alternate rounds; first round increase opposite the primrose point, and next time betwixt the points, and the last time opposite the points. You now continue working without increasing until you have ten rounds done from the points.

Take your darkest shade of green and work a round, then one round in open crochet of each shade until you come to the lightest; work again up to the darkest.

Now take the purple and work again in the

double crochet stitch. Work two rounds, put in the primrose, and work every thirteenth stitch of it.

Every succeeding round work an additional primrose stitch until you have eight primrose and five purple stitches. Finish with one round of purple.

Sew a long tassel and button to the top.

L.—BLUE BONNET FOR A LITTLE BOY.

It will require half an ounce of bright shaded blue, and a quarter of an ounce of shaded scarlet. Steel needle, No. 12.

It is all worked of the double crochet stitch.

Make a chain of three loops, join them, and

work round, putting two stitches into every chain stitch for the two first rounds. Every round afterwards you put two into every second stitch, then two into every third, then into every fourth; so on, increasing the distance of one betwixt each increase on every round, until you have it large enough, which it will be when about ten inches in diameter.

You now commence to decrease by missing a stitch, and do so as many stitches distant from each other as your last increase; and every round you make your decreases one stitch nearer each other, until you have worked twelve rounds from where you commenced to decrease.

You now take your scarlet and work ten rows back and forward (not round), so as to form the open. Finish with two rows of blue.

It will require to be made up with a strong lining. Sow a tassel and button to the top, and tie the open with a blue ribbon.

LI.—COVER FOR A ROUND PINCUSHION.

Boar's Head cotton, No. 36.

Make three loops, join them, and work round in double stitch, increasing every two stitches the first two rounds, then increase every three, and then every four, until you have a round an inch across. You then work an open round, taking up only every other stitch, and make three chain stitches betwixt each open one, then work one round of the double stitch.

Then a round of open, same as the first open round. Another open round, putting the needle into the large hole, and making four chain stitches betwixt each long stitch.

Then work two rounds again of the double stitch. Next round make two long stitches close together; then make three chain stitches, then your two long stitches again, missing a stitch betwixt every two. When you have joined your round, make a chain of seven loops, and begin the next round, which is the same as the last, only putting your two stitches into the large hole, then make your three loops. Another round the same. Now work three rounds of the double stitch.

It will now be large enough. You now work a border for the side of the cushion. Work it of the open stitch, but make two chain stitches betwixt each open stitch, and leave two stitches betwixt each on the work. You work three rounds the same. In working the last round, you only make one chain stitch betwixt each.

You now work a border to hang over the side. You work it to the plain part above the side. Make a chain of seven loops, and catch it in to the work, betwixt each open stitch. Work three rounds the same, but join the chain to the centre of last chain.

Make your cushion of coloured silk, and your cover slips over it. It will require no fastening, but drawing in with a ribbon at the bottom.

LII.—SHENILLE BAG.

Six shades of amber shenille.

Make thirty loops with the darkest; work an open row on each side. It is worked of the open crochet stitch throughout.

Work one round of each shade, and two of the lightest, then work one of each again, ending with the darkest shade. You line it with black or white satin; add rings and tassels to match.

LIII.—RIBBON FOR THE NECK.

Three shades of pink Berlin wool, three skeins of each shade, and three skeins of white will be required.

Commence with white. Make one hundred and sixty loops, work a row on each side of the chain with the white. It is all worked of the common open stitch.

Work one row all round of the lightest shade, then a round of the next shade, and one of the darkest. You put two stitches into every hole in turning round the ends, to make the work lie flat.

You work a slide of the darkest shade. Make twenty-six loops, join them together, and continue working round the double stitch until you have two inches worked.

You pass the ends of the ruff through the cross way.

LIV.—TURKISH SCARF FOR THE NECK.

It looks well of shaded amber, and royal blue Berlin wool.

Make a chain of two hundred and fifty loops. Work two rows of double crochet.

Change your colour and work three long crochet stitches close together, lifting every loop, then a chain of three loops. Repeat the three long stitches, leaving three loops betwixt the last three long stitches.

Every row after the first you work your three long stitches into the large hole. Continue working in the same manner until you have it a quarter of a yard broad, changing your colour every row.

You finish with two rows of double crochet, to make both edges correspond.

Add shenille tassels and an ivory slide.

LV.—SMALL HANDKERCHIEF.

It will require half an ounce of white, and four shades of scarlet, for the border, two skeins of each shade, and four skeins of the second shade for the fringe.

Stitch the long crochet with two chain stitches between each long stitch.

Commence with white. Make a chain of six loops, join them, put three stitches into the large hole. Make four chain stitches at the commencement of every row.

Every row after you put two stitches into the first, middle, and last stitches.

When you have eighteen rows done, you take the lightest scarlet, and work one row of each shade. When you have the darkest in, shade back to the lightest, then work one row of white to finish.

Cut the fringe into proper lengths, say five inches. Put three threads together, and draw it through with your crochet needle. Make one stitch to fasten it.

LVI.—WARM HANDKERCHIEF FOR THE HOUSE.

To be worked of double Berlin, and of the same stitch as the small handkerchief. You will require four ounces for the middle, and two ounces for the border and fringe.

You work three and a half ounces into the middle, one ounce into the border, and half an ounce same as the middle to finish. Then add the fringe of the same colour as the border.

LVII.—SCARF OF DIAMOND PATTERN.

It will require one ounce of shaded scarlet

single Berlin, and a steel crochet needle, No. 12. Make a chain five nails long. First row you work a chain of five loops, join it with two double crochet stitches to every third and fourth chain stitch. Every row afterwards you make a chain of five, and join it to the two centre stitches of the chain in the former row. When a yard and half long, work three rows of double crochet up each side. Draw up the ends, and add tassels and a slide.

LVIII.—COLLAR OF BERLIN WOOL.

Primrose and purple make a pretty contrast. Use a steel needle. No. 14.

Make a chain of one hundred and ten loops, stitch the long crochet. Work the chain and first row of the purple, the next four of primrose.

First Row.
Make two stitches close together, then a chain of two loops; miss a chain stitch betwixt every two long stitches.

Second Row.
Same as the first.

Third Row.
Same, but make three chain stitches betwixt every two long stitches.

Fourth Row.
Same as the third.

Fifth Row.
Same, only make four chain stitches instead of three. All the following rows you work round the ends.

Sixth Row.

Same as the last row, but with purple, and work round the ends.

Seventh Row.

Primrose. Work five long stitches into every hole, and two chain stitches betwixt every five long stitches.

Eighth Row.

Work two long stitches into every hole, and eight chain stitches betwixt every two long stitches.

Ninth Row.

Purple. Work one row of double crochet, which completes the collar.

Draw a ribbon round the neck; finish with a bow in front.

LIX.—COLLAR FOR A CHILD,
OF PRIMROSE AND PINK BERLIN.

Work it the common open stitch, but make a chain of two loops betwixt each stitch.

Commence with pink. Make a chain of twenty-four loops.

First Row.
Work round each side, putting three stitches into each end stitch.

Second Row.
Put two stitches into every other hole, and one into the other.

Third Row.
Put two stitches into every third hole, and one into each of the other holes.

Fourth Row.

Put two stitches into every sixth hole, and one into the others.

Fifth Row.

Put two stitches into every seventh hole, and one into the others.

Sixth Row.

You only increase in working round the ends in the following rows. You put two into every hole in working round the ends.

You work the seventh row of pink, only along one side, to make the under side broader than the upper.

You now work one row all round of primrose.

Work a string of the chain stitch, draw it through the middle; add tassels of the primrose also.

LX.—GAITERS FOR A LITTLE BOY.

Six skeins of black and fourteen of fawn colour Berlin will be required. Use an ivory needle. Work in double crochet stitch.

Make a chain of fifty loops of black, join it, and work three rounds.

Take the fawn and work twelve rounds.

You now take in by missing a stitch in every other round until you have taken in five times.

You then work seven rounds. For the instep part, you work back and forward on one half of the leg, going a stitch in on every row until you have nine rows done.

You now tie on the black and work three

rounds. When done, work a row of single crochet up the outside of the leg of black, and two rows of double crochet.

Sew four small black buttons up the side to make it appear as if buttoned up. You sew a strap to one side, and button it on the other.

LXI.—LADY'S SLIPPER.

An ounce and half of shaded double Berlin will be required. Purple or scarlet looks well.

It is done the double crochet stitch, only you put your needle into the edge of the work furthest from you, so as to make the work sit up in ridges.

Make a chain of fourteen loops, work back and forward until you have a piece long enough to go round the heel part of the shoe.

You now make a chain of thirty loops, sixteen being for the instep, and fourteen for the other side.

You now work back and forward across the whole, and will have forty-four stitches in all.

You then commence taking in after the first row, by missing the middle stitch.

When you have worked enough for the front of the shoe you crochet the heel part to the side of the front, and sew a fringe round the top, which you can do, by winding the wool round a mesh, and sewing it on; it requires two rows.

You can make them very neatly up yourself, by buying a pair of cork soles, (same as are worn inside shoes,) and sewing your work to the edge of the sole. Draw a ribbon round the instep to tie in front.

—:❊:—

LXII.—DARY'S BOOTS.

Primrose and white look well; it will require four skeins of white and six of primrose; use a steel crochet needle, No. 10. Commence with primrose, make forty-eight loops, join them and work one round, then work seven rounds of white of the double crochet stitch.

Work one round of open, then work of the double crochet stitch four rows, but only on twelve stitches, and work back and forward, then take your primrose and work seven rows in the same manner, which finishes the instep; you now work along the sides of the instep and round the heel part, when you have done seven rows, close the sole by working both together; the same at the toe. The sole will be a little fuller than the upper part, but full it in a little so as not to make the toe too broad; work a string of the chain stitch, and draw it through the open row

---

LXIII.—BABY'S SHOE.

Of shaded single Berlin; use a steel needle; No. 16: work it the same stitch as the lady's slipper, you commence at the toe, make a chain of twelve stitches, increase a stitch in the middle of every row until you have eighteen rows done.

You now only work your rows twelve stitches long for the heel part; work thirty rows, join it to the front part, work one row of single crochet round the top, to work a frill into.

You work the frill of an open stitch, place the wool round the needle, draw the wool through the work, then through two loops, again through two, then make a chain of two loops.

After you have one frill done, work another into the other side of the chain stitch.

Band to button round the ankle; make a chain of forty-five loops, work a row of double crotchet on each side, make a loop of six stitches for the button hole, sew it to the heel of the shoe.

Draw a ribbon round and tie it in front, make the sole of fine leather and bind it with ribbon, sew it to the work.

LXIV.—JUG STAND.

You require three colours of shaded double Berlin; purple, amber, and green, make a good contrast; needle No. 14.

Commence with green; it is all worked the double crochet stitch.

Make a chain of three loops, join them, and continue working round, increasing by putting two stitches into one. The first two rounds you increase in every stitch, on the third round in every second stitch, and on the fourth every third stitch; so on, in every round making your increases always one stitch further apart.

Work six rounds of green, five of purple, and four of the amber. For

THE BORDER

Make a chain of eight with green, join it to the work on the sixth stitch, then work a round of purple, in double crotchet.

Lace a piece of shaded amber chenille through the scollops.

LIV.—BIRD NEST FLOWER STAND.

You require two colours, say scarlet and white, four skeins of white and six of scarlet.

Make three loops, join them, and put two stitches into each, of double crochet, then put a scarlet and a white stitch into each stitch; you carry on both threads at a time.

Second round you put two scarlet stitches into each scarlet stitch, and two white into each white one.

Every round after you put one scarlet into each scarlet stitch, but put two into the last stitch.

Same in doing the white, put one white into each white stitch, but two into the last. So on until you have six stitches of white and six of scarlet.

You now break off the white and work one round of scarlet.

You then work an open round, then another open round, putting the stitch into the large hole

You now work a round of double long crochet and put three stitches into each hole.

You take the white again, and work a round of long crochet, and put one stitch into each hole

To finish, work a chain of four loops, join it to the edge, eighteen open stitches from where it was tied on. Make another chain of four loops, join it to the edge other eighteen stitches distant, so on until you have gone all round, it will now be drawn into a small circle, give the work betwixt each chain a turn over to the outside to make it sit neatly. Work a row of double crochet into all the chains of four to finish.

LXVI.—FLOWER STAND WITH FRILL.

Two colours of shaded Berlin. Amber and purple look pretty.

Commence with the purple, make three loops, join them and work round. The first round you increase by putting two stitches into one, you work the centre piece of single crochet.

The second round you increase every two stitches, the third round every three stitches, the fourth round every four stitches, the fifth round every fifth stitch; so on until your centre piece is large enough, you work the last four rounds of amber.

You now tie on your purple and work an open round.

Then another open round of purple, lifting every stitch to make it sit full.

You now work an open round of amber, lifting every stitch.

LXVII.—TOILET COVER.

Dutch twist No. 16, steel needle No. 14.

Make a chain of twenty-five loops, work in double crochet back and forward (and when you work in this manner you must always make a chain stitch at the end of the row, otherwise your work would decrease, as you cannot put your needle into the last stitch when you turn your rows) until you have a square, it will take twenty-five rows.

Sew the squares together and put a small tuft of cotton at each corner where they meet. Work an edge from any of the lace patterns and sew round.

This pattern answers for a bed quilt when wrought of much coarser cotton.

LXVIII.—BONNET CAP.

You will require three skeins of white Berlin wool, and three shades of scarlet, two skeins of the lightest shade, five skeins of the middle shade, and six of the last.

Commence with white, make a chain of one hundred loops, work round each side in open crochet stitch, until you have it seven rows wide, always letting out at each end by putting two stitches into one hole; round the end to make it lie flat.

You now work a round of the darkest shade; then a round of the lightest shade, in working this round you put your stitch into every chain stitch instead of the large hole, you do so for a finger length at each end, and half way round the end to make a fulness for the border.

You now work a round with your second shade, but on the full part you catch the wool twice round the needle to make a longer loop, and put the stitch into every chain stitch, on the full part; the back, and middle of the front, are done of the open stitch same as the other rounds.

You end with the darkest shade, and work the round same as the last.

Draw a scarlet ribbon down the centre, bring it out under the border.

LIX.—TOQUE.

Geranium colour and white look well. Commence with white, make a chain half a yard long, you then work a row of triple long open stitch, that is, put the wool three times round the needle, and then draw the wool through two loops at a time until all are worked off, then make one loop, you miss every other chain stitch.

You now take your coloured wool and work of the common open stitch two rows round the white, putting four stitches into the end to make it sit flat.

You then work two rows of white, then two of the coloured, then one of white, and end with two rows of the coloured wool. You put two stitches into one in working round the ends to make it sit flat.

Draw a satin ribbon through the wide row in the centre; when worn you turn back the front part a little.

Put a rosette on each side, made either of crochet work or ribbon.

—⁂—

LXX.—VERY BEATIFUL TURKISH TIDDY.

It requires one ounce of gold colour Berlin wool, three skeins of each of the other colours, arranged in the following manner:—light blue, rose colour, light green, white, purple, white, dark green, dark red, dark blue.

A stripe of the gold colour is worked of double crochet stitch betwixt each colour. Three rows are sufficient.

You work all the three skeins into each stripe, as the colour is not repeated. It will be about a nail broad. You work them in the diamond hole pattern and the square hole pattern alternately.

The diamond is done in the following manner. Make a chain of four loops, join it to the gold colour every third stitch, work two double crochet stitches. The following rows you join your chain of four to the two centre stitches of the chain in the former row.

Square Hole.

Make three long crochet stitches into three

stitches on the work, then a chain of three loops, again the three long stitches, passing three chain stitches on the work. The following rows you put your three long stitches into the hole.

You commence and end with three rows of double crochet.

BORDER OF GOLD COLOUR.

Work three rows of double crochet at each side.

You then make a chain of seven loops; join it to the work on every fifth stitch. Another round the same.

Last Round.

Make a chain of seven, join it to the centre of the chain in the last round. You then work double crochet up to the centre of the next loop, which will take six stitches. You then make your chain of seven loops; so on all round.

LXXI.—ROUND PURSE.

This purse has a star on each side, and requires two colours of medium size purse twist. Rose colour and blue make a pretty contrast. You will require two skeins of blue and one of rose colour.

You carry on both your colours at once, and work in double crochet.

Commence with the blue, and make a chain of three, join them, put two into each stitch until you have ten stitches.

You now put in your rose colour, and put one rose colour stitch and one blue stitch into each stitch.

Next round you put two blue into each blue, and two rose colour into each rose colour.

Every round afterwards you put two stitches into the last rose colour stitch. Always put one blue into each blue, so as never to have more than two blue stitches. You continue working in this manner until you have eight rose colour stitches.

You now put two blue stitches into the last rose colour stitch. By that means your rose colour will get less every row, and your blue will increase.

When you have come to one rose colour stitch, you work two rounds entirely of blue.

One side will now be done. You work another side in the same manner to correspond. Crochet them together, leaving enough open to sew on the top. It must be a semicircle one. Sew two rows of loops of beads round; twist one row round the other

This pattern looks very pretty with the star formed of beads. You string your beads on the rose colour, and put one forward every time you make a rose colour stitch.

LXXII.—LONG PURSE, WITH BEADS,
SCARLET AND GOLD.

You will require four skeins of purse twist, and one bunch of beads.

String on a few beads, then commence. Make a chain five nails long.

Work in long crochet. Place your silk round the needle, put your needle into every other chain stitch, draw the silk through, then through one loop, through two, again through two. You now put forward a bead, then draw the silk through one loop.

Every row after the first you put your needle through the large hole.

You cut off your silk at the end of each row, and commence at the other end, so as your beads may be all on one side.

You crochet up one third at each end, draw in the ends, and add gilt tassels and slide.

LXXIII.—STRIPED PURSE.

You require two skeins of blue and two of fawn colour. Work a steel needle, No. 20.

Commence with the fawn colour. Make a chain ten inches long; work six rows of double crochet.

Take the blue, and after you have joined it to the work, make a chain of five loops, and join it to the work on every fourth stitch. Next row you join the chain to the centre stitch of the chain in the last row, with a double crochet stitch.

When you have worked four open rows, you work one row with only three stitches in the chain instead of five. You now take the fawn colour and work six rows of double crochet. This forms an open and a close stripe. You can put a pattern of beads on the third stripe if you wish. String your beads before you commence, and put one forward before you draw the thread through the work. This purse is made up as the last.

LXXIV.—SHORT PURSE.

This purse has a star at the bottom, and spots throughout.

You require two colours, say pink and green—two skeins of green, and one of pink.

Make a chain of three with the green, join them, and put two stitches into each. You now take the pink and work with both colours. Put one green and one pink into each stitch. You will have six of each. Next row you put two green into each green, and two pink into each pink. Every row afterward put one green into each green, and one pink into each pink, but put two stitches into the last pink one, until you have fourteen pink stitches. You now put a green stitch into the last pink stitch. This will lessen your pink and increase your green. When your pink is reduced to one, you continue a round entirely of green, and then commence making your spots. You put one pink stitch in the centre betwixt each point; next round you put two pink; next three; next two; next one; then a round entirely of green. The next spot you place betwixt these in the former rounds. When nearly as deep as you wish, you must leave an open at each side to admit the top being sewed neatly on. In working the open, you must cut off your silk, and begin at the half, and only work one side up at a time. When you have worked six rows, or as many as the depth of your top requires, you cut off your silk, and work the other half to correspond.

———◆※◆———

LXXV.—THE STAR WINE RUBBER.

You work them in shaded scarlet Berlin wool, and No. 14 Dutch twist. Use a steel needle, No. 20.

Commence with the scarlet, make a chain of three, join it and work round in double crochet, putting two stitches into every chain stitch until you have nine stitches round. You now put in the white; keep both threads and let one pass on the wrong side.

First Round.

Put a white stitch, and a scarlet one into every chain stitch.

Second Round.

Put two scarlet stitches into each scarlet one, and one white stitch into each white one.

Third Round.

Put one white into each white one, and a scarlet stitch into each scarlet one, but increase on the last stitch of each scarlet point. You should have nine points. Continue working every round the same as this, until you have eight scarlet stitches on each point.

You now put two white stitches into every last scarlet stitch in each point, and put the white over the white, and the scarlet over the scarlet, as in the former rounds. Continue working in this manner until you have all white stitches; you then work two rounds entirely of white.

You now tie on the scarlet and commence

THE BORDER.

First Round.

Work all round of double crochet stitch.

Second Round.

Work seven double crochet stitches, then make a chain of seven loops, miss three chain stitches on the work, then the seven double crochet again.

Third Round.

Put a long stitch into each of the seven chain stitches in the last round, and put a long stitch into the centre of the seven double crochet stiches; make a chain stitch between each long stitch.

Last Round.

Make a chain of four, join it into the open between each long stitch with a double crochet stitch.

LXXVI.—LARGE ROUND STAND.

WITH A FRILL.

It will require half an ounce of shaded scarlet single Berlin, four skeins of single white, and half an ounce of white double Berlin. Commence with scarlet.

Make three chain stitches, join them, and work

three rounds, putting two stitches into every chain stitch to increase.

Fourth Round.

Open crochet.

Fifth Round.

Put three double long stitches into every open, and make one chain stitch between every three long stitches.

Sixth Round.

Take the white single Berlin, and make five chain stitches, join them to the work in the open between each three long stitches, with a single crochet stitch.

Seventh Round.

Make five chain stitches, join them to the centre of the five chain stitches in the last round.

P

Eighth Round.

Same as the seventh.

Ninth Round.

Take the scarlet, put four double long stitches into every large hole.

Tenth Round.

Put one long stitch into every chain stitch.

Eleventh Round.

Take the white, make a chain of five, join it to the work by a single crochet stitch on every fourth chain stitch.

Twelfth Round.

Same as the eleventh.

Thirteenth Round.

Take the scarlet, put three long stitches into

every open, make one chain stitch between each long stitch.

Fourteenth Round.

Take the white double Berlin, put two double long crochet stitches into every open, and make two chain stitches between each double long stitch.

Last Round.

Take the scarlet, put one long stitch into every open, and make two chain stitches betwixt each long one.

—✛✕✚—

LXXVII.—CHINCHILLA MUFF.

It will require two ounces of shaded grey double Berlin.

Make a chain half a yard long, join it, and work in double crochet stitch, but catch the wool round the needle and insert your needle into the under side of the chain; draw the thread through the work, then through the three loops on the needle; continue working in the same stitch until you have it as long as you wish it.

Stuff it and line it according to taste.

LXXVIII.—ANTI MACASSAR.

DIAMOND PATTERN.

Worked in No. 16 Dutch twist.

Make a chain half a yard long. Before commencing each row you make five chain stitches to raise it up the height of the row.

First Row

Put four long into four successive chain stitches, make two chain stitches, then the four long stitches again, missing two chains.

Second Row.

Put three long stitches into the first three chain stitches, * make two chain stitches, put a long stitch into the open, make two chains, then eight long stitches. Repeat from * until the row is finished.

Third Row.

Put two long stitches into the first two chain stitches, * make two chain stitches, put a long stitch into the open, again two chain stitches, one long into the open, two chains, then six long stitches into six successive chain stitches, over the eight long stitches in the last row. Repeat from * until the row is finished.

Fourth Row.

Put two long stitches into the two first chain stitches, * then put a long stitch into each open, with two chain stitches between each long one, and four long stitches above the six in the last row. Repeat from * until the row is finished.

Fifth Row.

Put a long stitch into every open, with two chain stitches betwixt each long stitch then put two long stitches above the four in the last row. Repeat.

Sixth Row.

A long stitch into every open, with two chain stitches between each long stitch.

Seventh Row.

Put a long stitch into each open, with a chain of two between each long stitch; but put two long stitches into the open opposite the point of the last diamond.

Eighth Row.

This row is the same as the fourth, only the four long stitches that are together, will be over the two in the last row.

Ninth Row.

This is the same as the third row; the six close stitches coming opposite the four in the last row.

Tenth Row.

Same as the second.

Commence again at the first row, and work

until it is as long as you require it; then work the border all round.

BORDER.

First Round.

Long crochet quite close together all round.

Second Round.

Make seven double crochet stitches, then a chain of seven, then seven double crochet again, missing five chain stitches on the work.

Third Round.

Seven double crochet stitches over the open, then a chain of seven.

Fourth Round.

One long stitch into each of the seven chain stitches in the last row, with one chain stitch between each long stitch, and put one long stitch into the centre of the double crochet stitches in the last round.

Last Round.

Make a chain of four and join it into every open between each long stitch in the last round with a double crochet stitch.

―✦―

LXXIX.—ANTI MACASSAR.

WAVE PATTERN.

Dutch Twist No. 16, Needle No. 18.

Make a chain half a yard in length. Before

commencing each row you make five chain stitches to raise the row up.

First Row.

A long stitch into every third chain stitch, and make two chain stitches between each long one.

Second Row.

Put a long stitch into the two first holes, and make two chain stitches between each long one, * then put two long ones into the third hole, and one long stitch into each of the next four holes. Repeat from * until the row is finished, and make your row end with two single long stitches after the two that are close together.

Third Row.

Put a long stitch into the first hole, * then put

four long stitches into four successive chain stitches, they must be put over the two close ones in the last row, then put three long stitches into the next three holes, making a chain of two between each long stitch. Repeat from the * until the row is finished.

Fourth Row.

Put one long stitch into the first hole, then make two chain stitches, * put six long stitches into six successive chain stitches, two chains and a long one into the next two holes. Repeat from the * until the row is finished.

Fifth Row.

Eight long stitches into eight successive chain stitches over the six close stitches in the last row, two chain stitches, one long stitch into the middle hole, then two chain stitches. Repeat.

Sixth Row.

Put four long stitches in four successive chain stitches, make two chain stitches, miss two chains on the work. Repeat.

Seventh Row.

Three long into the first three chain stitches, * make two chain stitches, put a long stitch into the open, again two chain stitches, and then eight long stitches into eight successive chain stitches. Repeat from the * until the row is finished.

Eighth Row.

Put two long stitches into the two first chain stitches, * make two chain stitches, a long stitch

CROCHET WORK.   191

into each open, with two chain stitches between each, two chain stitches, then put six long stitches over the eight long in the last row. Repeat from the * until the row is finished.

Ninth Row.

Put two long stitches into the two first chain stitches, * make two chain stitches and put a long stitch into each hole, with two chain stitches between each long one, two chains, then four long stitches above the six close ones in the last row. Repeat from the * until the row is finished.

Tenth Row.

Put a long stitch into the first chain stitch. * A long stitch into each open, with two chain stitches between each, then put two long stitches in the centre above the four long stitches in the last row. Repeat from the * until the row is finished.

Eleventh Row.

Put a long stitch into each open, and make two chain stitches between each long stitch.

Commence again at the second row, and repeat the pattern until as large as you wish; always observing that you make the point of the wave opposite the last point.

BORDER.

First Row.

Long stitches close together all round.

Second Row.
Open crochet.

Third Row.
Long crochet close together.

Fourth Row.
Seven double crochet stitches into seven successive chain stitches, then make seven chain stitches, again the seven double stitches, missing four chain stitches on the work.

Fifth Row.
Put five double crochet stitches over the seven in the last row, make a chain of seven, and join it to the centre of the chain in the last row,

again seven chain stitches, then the five double crochet stitches.

Sixth Row.

Put three double crochet stitches above the five in the last row, then make a chain of five, and join it to the top of the chain in the last row, one stitch from the former join; again a chain of five and join it to the other side of the former join, then again a chain of five, then your three double crochet stitches.

Last Row

Double crochet.

LXXX.—DREAD BASKET NAPKIN.

Boar's Head cotton, No. 10; needle, No. 16; Bell Gauge.

Make a chain three half-quarters long.

Make a chain of four at the commencement of every row, to raise it up the height of the row.

First Row.

Put five long stitches into five successive chain stitches, and make one chain stitch between each five long stitches.

Second Row.

Put three long stitches in the centre of the five in the last row, and make a chain of three between each three long stitches, and miss three chains on the work.

Third Row.

Put a long stitch in the centre of the three long stitches in the last row, and put one in the centre of the three chain stitches in the last row, and make two chain stitches between each long stitch.

Commence again at the first row, but always observe that you place your five long stitches above the five long stitches in the last row. Repeat the pattern until you have it half a yard long. You then commence the border.

BORDER.
First Round.

Long crochet all round, but, in turning the corners, put two stitches into each chain stitch.

Second Round.

A long stitch into every third chain stitch, and make two chain stitches between each long stitch.

Third Round.

Long crochet into every chain stitch.

Fourth Round.

Put six double crochet stitches into six successive chain stitches, then make a chain of five, and again the six double crochet stitches, but miss two chain stitches on the work.

Fifth Round.

Put three double crochets in the centre of the six, then make six chain stitches, and join them to the centre of the chain in the last row, with a long stitch; then make other six chain stitches, and again the three double crochet stitches in the centre of the six.

Sixth Round.

Make a chain of six loops, and join to the work with a long stitch, opposite the long stitch in the last row; then make another chain of six, and join it with a long stitch to the centre of the three double crochet stitches in the last row.

LXXXI.—COLLAR.

SPIDER NET PATTERN.
(See Engraving, No. 8.)

Boar's Head cotton, No. 40; needle, No. 24; Bell Gauge.

Make a chain half a yard long.

First Row.

Long crochet into every chain stitch.

Second Row

Make a chain of eight loops, join them to the work on every fifth chain with a double crochet stitch.

Third Row.

Make a chain of eight loops, join them to the fourth chain stitch in the chain in the last row; then make four chain stitches, and join them to the next chain stitch; you again make other eight chain stitches, and join them in the same manner to the fourth chain stitch of the next chain

You work other six rows in the same manner as the third.

You now break off the thread, and tie it on at

the neck and work round each end in working the border.

BORDER.

First Row.

Put four long stitches into the end of the first row; then put four long stitches into four successive chain stitches on the work; make two chain stitches between every four long stitches, and miss one chain between each four long stitches.

Second Row.

Put a long stitch into every open, and make four chain stitches between each long stitch.

Third Row.

Put four long stitches into every open, and make two chain stitches between each four long stitches.

Fourth Row.

Make seven chain stitches, join them into the open between the four long stitches in the last row; then make four chain stitches, and join them into the same open with a double crochet stitch.

Fifth Row.

Make a chain of four stitches; join them to the centre of the chain of seven in the last row. Make another chain of four, and join them to the centre of the four chain stitches in the last row.

Sixth Row.

Make a chain of seven stitches, and join them to the point where the chain was joined to the centre of the seven in the former row.

Last Row.

Double crochet into every chain stitch.

LXXXII.—COMFORTABLE PRUDENCE CAP.

It will require three shades of scarlet, and white Use a No. 14 ivory needle.

Commence with the darkest shade. Make a chain half a yard long, join it, and work two rounds of double crochet.

You now take the second shade, and work one row in open crochet, but leave twenty chain stitches for the neck part.

You now tie on your lightest shade, and work one row, and put two stiches into the last hole. You continue putting two stitches into the last hole in every row until finished.

You now work a white row.

You take the darkest shade, and repeat the

colours in the same manner, until you have five stripes.

You now work two rounds of double crochet stitch, working along each side and round the neck part.

Plait a string, and draw it down the first row of holes to tie under the chin.

LXXXIII.—OPERA CAP.
(See Engraving.)
SQUARE AT THE EARS.

Rose colour and white Berlin wool. It will require half an ounce of each colour.

Work with needles No. 15 and No. 10.

CROCHET WORK.

Commence with the rose colour, and use No 15 needle. Make a chain a little more than half a yard long.

The first row you put three long stitches into one chain stitch, make one chain stitch between each three, and miss three chains betwixt each three long stitches.

Every row after the first you put the three long stitches into the open between the three long stitches in the last row.

You make a white and coloured row alternately, until you have five coloured rows and four white rows, you then work a row all round of double crochet.

You now take the white, and commence the border, and use needle No. 10.

You work it in double long crochet stitch; put two stitches in each chain stitch, and make one chain stitch between each long stitch.

You put two stitches into each chain stitch only round the ends, and about a fourth part up the front on each side. Put only one stitch into each chain stitch along the top.

You finish with a row of rose colour; put a double crochet stitch into each open, and make three chain stitches between each double stitch.

You now make two rosettes in the following manner, and sew one on each side:—

Make a chain of twenty loops with the rose colour, then put two double long stitches into each chain stitch, and make two chain stitches between each long stitch. Finish with a white row; putting a double crochet stitch into each open

CROCHET WORK.

and make three chain stitches between each double stitch, then draw it up.

Plait a string with the wool, and make a tassel at the end. Sew one on at each end.

———❊———

LXXXIV.—ELEGANT OPERA CAP.
(See Engraving.)

It will require half an ounce of shaded amber Berlin wool, and six skeins of white. Use a No. 14 crochet needle.

Commence with white; make a chain not quite half a yard long.

First Row.
Open crochet.

Second Round.

Take the amber, and work along each side of the white. Put a long stitch into every chain stitch, for a finger length up each side. Put a double crochet stitch into every other chain stitch, and make a chain stitch betwixt each double stitch, along each side of the middle part.

Third Round.

Put a long stitch into each chain stitch round each end, and up each side, but put two into each in turning the end, and then work along the middle part in the same manner as the last round.

Fourth Round.

Same as the last, but commence the double crochet stitches three or four stitches nearer the ends.

Fifth Round.

Same as the last.

Sixth Round.

Take the white, and commence the Frill. Put two double long stitches into each chain stitch round each end, and half-way up the broad part. The remainder of the broad part you put one single long stitch into each chain stitch, and along the narrow part you put a long stitch into every other chain stitch, with a chain stitch betwixt each long stitch.

Finish with a double crochet row of the amber. Draw a ribbon down the open row in the centre.

LXXXV.—CARRIAGE CAP

It will require three shades of blue, three skeins of the darkest, six of the next shade, and half an ounce of the lightest, and three quarters of an ounce of white. Work with a needle No. 12.

Commence with white. Make a chain three half quarters long—work a row of open crochet. You then take the lightest blue, and work round each side of the white, and put four stitches into the end of the white.

Next round, take the middle shade, and work all round, putting two stitches into the end stitches to make it lie flat.

You now take the darkest shade, and work all round in the same manner as the last round. You then take the middle shade, and work all round, then the lightest, and work in the same manner also. You now work a round of double crochet of the same shade.

You now take the white, and commence

THE BORDER.

First Round.

Put a double long stitch into every chain stitch, and make two chain stitches between each long stitch.

Second Round.

Take the lightest shade of blue, make a chain of four stitches, and join them into every open with a double crochet stitch.

Last Round.

Take the white and make four chain stitches,

CROCHET WORK. 211

and join them into the chain in the last row with a double crochet stitch.

You now tie the white on the Cap, a half-quarter up from the end, and two stripes from the Border. Work round the end on the stripe in the same manner as the Border, putting two stitches into the space between the stitches on the row. You work another frill on the second stripe from the last, round the end in the same manner, so as to form three borders round the ears.

You plait a string, and draw it down the centre of the Cap, and let the string come out below the frill to tie under the chin.

LXXXVI.—LADY'S POLKA.
WITH AN ERMINE BORDER.
(See Frontispiece.)

You will require ten ounces of double Berlin wool,—claret looks well—two ounces of white, and half an ounce of black for the Border. Work with an ivory needle No. 10.

BODY.

It is all wrought the double crochet stitch, always remembering to make a chain stitch before you commence the rows, to keep it straight at the edge.

You commence at the waist, make a chain of one hundred loops, or as many as will go round the waist. Work twenty rows, but on the tenth row you commence letting out for the gusset In front; do so by putting two stitches into one every other row a finger length from each end.

When you have twenty rows wrought, you commence the back.

Work sixteen rows on the fifty middle stitches, leaving an equal number at each end for the fronts. When you have the sixteen rows wrought, you begin to slope at the shoulders, which you do by *not* working the last stitch on the row, and by *not* making the chain stitch before you commence the rows. You work twelve rows after you begin the slope; you then break off your thread, and tie it on to work the front part.

You continue the increase at the gusset for other six rows, work sixteen rows from where you tied on the thread, then commence the slope at the throat, which you do in the same manner as the slope at the shoulder. When you have other twelve rows done, break off the thread, and work the other front to correspond.

You now work the jacket part. Tie on the thread at the waist, and work twenty-six rows, making it round at the ends, which you do by *not making* the chain stitch at the beginning of the row, and by commencing the rows on the second stitch.

You must let it out, to form the shape, on every third row; do so by putting two stitches into every fourteenth stitch.

You now sew the shoulders together, and commence

THE BORDER.

Tie on the white, and work two rows all round, then place in the black, and work a round, carrying on both threads at the same time, and work six stitches with white, and two with black.

You then work a round all white.

Then one with six stitches white and two black, placing the two black stitches betwixt the two black in the former row.

You then work another row all white.

Then one with the two black stitches in it, but place them above the first row with the black stitches.

You finish with two rows all white.

SLEEVE.

Make a chain of fifty loops, work fifty-four rows, and then commence the slope at the top, slope on both sides until it is nearly to a point, in the same manner as the slope at the shoulders.

Sew the sleeve together, and work the cuff; work all round, and in the same manner as the border round the body.

Sew in the sleeves.

LXXXVII.—CHILD'S POLKA.

The following dimensions will fit a child about three years old, and it can be wrought either in Fleecy or double Berlin wool.

It will require five ounces of royal blue, and two ounces of white, with half an ounce of black for the ermine border. Use a No. 10 Ivory needle. It is wrought in the same manner as the Lady's Polka.

Make a chain of eighty loops for the waist. Work ten rows; then commence the back, and work ten rows on the thirty-six middle stitches, leaving twenty-two at each end for the fronts. You then commence sloping at the shoulder, which you do by *not* making the chain stitch at the beginning of the rows, and by commencing each row on the second chain stitch; you work eight rows after you begin to slope.

You now tie on the thread at the bottom of the back, and work the front. Work ten rows, and then begin the slope at the throat, which you do in the same manner as the slope at the shoulder. You work six rows after you commence to slope.

You now tie on your thread at the other side of the back, and work the other front to correspond.

You work the jacket part in the same manner as the Lady's Polka, but work it only sixteen ows deep.

You now sew the shoulders together, and work the border in the same manner as Lady's also.

SLEEVES.

Make a chain of thirty-four loops. Work twenty rows; then begin the slope at the top, which you do in the same manner as the Lady's. Work a cuff at the bottom to correspond with the border; you join the sleeve, and work the cuff all round.

Sew in the sleeves.

LXXXVIII.—D'OYLEY.

FOR A SALVER OR BREAD PLATE

Boar's Head cotton, No. 12; needle, No. 16.

Make a chain of five loops, join them, and work round, always joining your rounds with a single crochet stitch.

First Round

Put two double crochet stitches into every chain stitch.

Second Round

Put a long crochet stitch into every chain stitch, and make two chain stitches between each long one.

Third Round.

Put a long crochet stitch into every chain stitch, and make one chain stitch between each long stitch.

Fourth Round.

Same as the third.

Fifth Round.

Make a chain of six loops; join them to the work with a double crochet stitch on every fifth chain stitch.

Sixth Round.

Put three long stitches into every open, and make two chain stitches betwixt each three long stitches.

Seventh Round.

Same as the sixth.

Eighth Round.

Put two double crochet stitches above the two chain stitches in the last row, and make four chain stitches, betwixt each two double crochet stitches.

Ninth Round.

Make a chain of six loops, and join them to the centre of the chain in the last row with a double crochet stitch.

Tenth Round.

Make a chain of eight loops, and join them to the middle of the chain in the last round with a double crochet stitch.

Eleventh Round.

Put three double crochet stitches in the four

middle stitches of the chain in the last round, and make five chain stitches between each four double crochet stitches.

Twelfth Round.
Double crochet into every chain stitch.

Thirteenth Round.
Double crochet also.

Fourteenth Round.
Put a long stitch into every other chain stitch, and make two chain stitches between each long stitch.

Fifteenth Round.
Double crochet.

Sixteenth Round.
Double crochet.

Seventeenth Round.
Same as the fourteenth.

Eighteenth and Nineteenth Rounds.
Double crochet.

Twentieth Round.
Make a chain of seven loops, then three double crochet stitches, missing four chain stitches on the work, between every three double crochet stitches.

Twenty-first Round.
Make a chain of seven loops, then put three double crochet stitches into the three middle stitches of the chain in the last round.

Twenty-second Round.
Same as the last round.

Twenty-third Round.

Same as the last round.

Twenty-fourth and twenty-fifth Rounds.

Double crochet.

Twenty-sixth Round.

Make a chain of ten loops, then three double crochet stitches, and miss seven chain stitches on the work, between each three double crochet stitches.

Twenty-seventh Round.

Make a chain of ten loops, and then three double crochet stitches, in the three middle stitches of the chain in the last round.

Twenty-eighth Round.

Same as the last.

Twenty-ninth Round.

Make a chain of six loops, and then put seven double crochet stitches, in the seven middle stitches of the chain in the last round.

Thirtieth Round.

Make a chain of nine loops, then put four double crochet stitches, into the four middle stitches of the chain in the last round.

Last Round.
Double crochet.

LXXXIX.—PRETTY SIMPLE SCARF

FOR A CHILD.

You will require half an ounce of pink, and half an ounce of grey. Use a No. 12 needle.

Make a chain three quarters of a yard long with the pink, and work two rows of double crochet.

You now take the grey, and work a row of open crochet.

You continue working in open crochet until you have it three nails broad, changing your colour every row.

You finish by working two rows of double crochet with pink.

Draw it up at the ends, and make a tassel of the two colours, and sew them on at the ends.

XC.—BAND FOR THE NECK.

You will require three skeins of white and three of scarlet.

Commence with scarlet; make a chain five half quarters long.

You work along each side of the chain with the scarlet; put a double crochet stitch into every second chain stitch, and make a chain stitch between each double stitch. You now take the white, and work two rows along each side in the same manner, putting the double stitch into the chain between the double stitch in the last row

You take the scarlet, and work round with it in the same manner to finish.

XCI—BLUE BONNET FOR HOLDING PENCE.

It will require two skeins of royal blue Berlin, one of white, and one of scarlet. Work with a steel needle, No. 18, and work it tight.

Commence with blue; make three chain stitches, join them, and work round, in double crochet, putting two stitches into each for the first three rounds; the fourth round you put two stitches into every second stitch; the fifth round you put two into every third; the sixth two into every fourth; the seventh round put two into every fifth stitch; the eighth round put two into every sixth stitch. The crown is now large enough; you then commence taking in, which you do in the following manner :—

There are four take-in rows; the first row you miss every sixth stitch, the next row miss every fifth stitch, next miss every fourth stitch, and the last row miss every third.

You now tie on the scarlet and white, and work two stitches of white and two of scarlet. The next round you put the scarlet stitches into the white stitches, and the white into the scarlet ones in the last round.

Work three rows in the same manner. You now tie on the blue, and work one round.

You make a little tuft of scarlet, and sew it on the top, and put a bow of narrow blue ribbon at the side.

XCII.—PEN WIPER.

Shaded amber and green Berlin wool.

Make a chain of three; join it and work round in double crochet, putting two into every stitch. The next round you work in long crochet, put two into every stitch; another round the same.

You now take the amber, and work a round, putting two stitches into one, and one into the next, all round.

You now work a round of green, putting two stitches into every third chain stitch, and one into each of the others.

The next row you make five chain stitches, and join them to the work with a double crochet stitch; on every third chain stitch, another double crochet stitch; then your chain again.

Finish with a double crochet row of amber.

You work another circle in the same manner, but of different colours.

Put three rounds of black linen between them, and fasten all together in the centre with a button.

XCII.—BEAUTIFUL UNDER SLEEVE.

Boar's Head cotton, No. 40; needle 24.

Make a chain a quarter of a yard long, join it, and work two rows, of open crochet.

Third Round.

Put a treble long crochet stitch into every

third chain stitch, and make two chain stitches between each long stitch.

Fourth Round.
Open crochet.

Fifth Round.
Open Crochet.

Sixth Round.
Put a double long stitch into every open, and make one chain stitch between each long stitch.

Seventh Round.
Same as the last.

Eighth Round.
Put five double long stitches into five successive opens, with one chain stitch between each long stitch, then make four chain stitches, then put a long stitch into the second open from

the five long stitches; again a chain of four, and commence your next five long stitches in the second hole from the single long stitch.

Ninth Round.

Put four double long stitches with one chain stitch between each, into the opens above the five long stitches in the last round, then make four chain stitches, and then put a long stitch on each side of the single long stitch in the last round, then make four chain stitches.

Tenth Round.

Put a double long stitch into each of the three opens, above the four long stitches in the last round; make one chain stitch between each long stitch, then make four chain stitches, and put a double long stitch, on each side of the two long stitches in the last round, and one double long stitch in the open between the two; again a chain of four.

Eleventh Round.

Put a double long stitch into each of the opens between the three long stitches, with a chain stitch between each long stitch, then four chain stitches, then put a double long stitch on each side of the next three long stitches, with a long stitch into each open between the long stitches in the last row; again four chain stitches.

Twelfth Round.

Put a long stitch into the open between the two double long stitches, then make four chain stitches, then one on each side of the four long stitches, and a long stitch into each open between the four, with a chain stitch between each long stitch, then four chain stitches.

Thirteenth Round.

Put a double long stitch, on each side of the five long stitches and one into each open, with a chain stitch between each long stitch, then make nine chain stitches.

Fourteenth Round.

Put a double long stitch, into each open between the six long stitches in the last round, then make four chain stitches, and put one double long stitch into the centre of the nine chain stitches; again four chain stitches.

Fifteenth Round.

Put a double long stitch into each open between the five long stitches, with one chain stitch between each long stitch, then make four chain stitches, then make a long stitch on each side of the single long stitch, again four chain stitches.

Sixteenth Round.

Put a double long stitch into each open between four long stitches, with one chain stitch between each long stitch, then make four chain stitches, then put a double long stitch on each side of the two long stitches with a long stitch into the open between the two, again four chain stitches.

Seventeenth Round.

Put a double long stitch into each open between the four long stitches, then make four chain stitches, then put a double long stitch on each side of the three long stitches, and one long stitch between each of the three, with a chain stitch between each long stitch, again four chain stitches.

Eighteenth Round.

Put a double long stitch into the open between the three, then make four chain stitches, then a double long stitch on each side, and one into each open of the four long stitches, again four chain stitches.

Nineteenth Round.

Put one double long stitch, between the two long stitches, then make four chain stitches, then put one long stitch on each side of the five long stitches, and one into each open between the five long stitches, with one chain between each long stitch, again four chain stitches.

Twentieth Round.

Put a double long stitch, into each open between the six long stitches, and two into the chain of four, with a chain stitch between each long stitch.

Twenty-first Round.

A double long stitch into each open, with one chain between each.

You now commence at the first round and work the pattern over once more.

Work at the bottom of the sleeve an edge from any of the patterns of edging given in this book.

Draw a ribbon in the long open row between the two rows of open crochet.

XCIV.—TRIMMING.

Which can be wrought in any kind of cotton suitable for the purpose you require it.

It is worked across in the same manner as knitted trimming.

Make a chain of twelve loops.

First Row.

Put a long stitch into the seventh chain stitch, make four chain stitches, another long stitch into the third chain stitch from the last long stitch, again four chain, then a long stitch into the last chain stitch, which completes the row.

Second Row.

Make four chain stitches, then put three long

stitches into the first hole, with a chain stitch between each, then three into the next hole in the same manner, which completes the row.

Third Row.

Make seven chain stitches, then put a long stitch into the second open, between the long stitches in the last row, then four chain stitches, again a long stitch into the second open from the last long stitch, then four chain stitches and a long stitch into the last open.

Commence again at the second row.

When you have worked as much as you require, work a row of open crochet along the straight side of the trimming to form a top.

XCV.—VANDYKE TRIMMING.

This pattern is also worked across in the same manner as knitted trimming.

First Row.

Make a chain of twenty-four loops, put a long stitch into the fifth chain stitch, then a long stitch into every other chain stitch, with a chain stitch between each, until you have six long stitches, then make four chain stitches, and put a long stitch into the last chain stitches, which completes the row.

Second Row.

Make four chain stitches, then put four long stitches into the large hole, with a chain stitch between each long stitch, you put a long stitch into the next four opens between the long stitches, with a chain stitch between each long stitch, which completes the row.

Third Row.

Make four chain stitches, then put a long stitch into six of the opens between the long stitches, with a chain stitch between each long stitch, then make four chain stitches, and put a long stitch into the last open, which finishes the row. Commence again at the second row.

When you have worked as much as you require, work a row of open crochet along the straight side to form a top.

EDINBURGH: PRINTED BY T. NELSON AND SONS.

www.ingramcontent.com/pod-product-compliance
Lightning Source LLC
Chambersburg PA
CBHW032010300426
44117CB00008B/973